MW01609520

MENTAL MASTERY
THE ALCHEMY OF THE MAGICKAL MIND

ABOUT THE AUTHOR

Gianmichael Salvato (Philadelphia, PA) is an Author, Naturopathic Physician, Anthropologist, Witch, Alchemist, Intersectional Feminist, Luciferian, Herbalist, and Animist. He's also the face and mind behind the Inner Alchemy Movement and The Collective.

As a lifelong hereditary Witch, drawing on more than fifty years of personal study and practice, Gianmichael's practice draws deeply from the well of Sacred Wisdom of the Ancestors and Spirits beyond the veil, as part of the Sicilian Craft of the Wise.

Gianmichael strives to live by these simple principles: personal responsibility, claiming his Power, speaking his truth (at all costs), living his truth (no matter the cost), following no creed, and always maintaining and respecting individual Sovereignty.

MENTAL MASTERY

THE ALCHEMY OF THE MAGICKAL MIND

By

Gianmichael Salvato

Morningstar Mediaworks & Publishing
Harrisburg, PA

Mental Mastery : The Alchemy of the Magickal Mind

Copyright © 2018 by Gianmichael Salvato. All rights reserved. No part of this book may be used or reproduced in any manner whatsoever, including Internet usage or reproduction, without express written permission from Morningstar Mediaworks & Publishing, except in the case of brief quotations embodied in critical articles, research, and reviews.

FIRST EDITION
First Printing, 2018

Cover design by Morningstar Mediaworks & Publishing

Library of Congress Cataloging-in-Publication Data
Names: Salvato, Gianmichael, author.
Title: Mental Mastery : The Alchemy of the Magickal Mind / by Gianmichael Salvato
Description: First Edition. | Harrisburg : Morningstar Mediaworks & Publishing, LLC |
Includes bibliographical references and index.
Identifiers: ISBN 978-0-359-70500-9 (alk. Paper)

Subjects: 1. Witchcraft | 2. Magic | 3. Folklore – Buddhist | 4. New Thought | 5. Buddhism

TABLE OF CONTENTS

INTRODUCTION

For many years, my classes and writing were systematically compartmentalized. Books, workshops, blog articles, and classes referring to the esoteric practices of Buddhism, Bön, and the Hindu philosophy were always written under my monastic "dharma name" – Gurudas Śunyatananda; while New Thought, occult and witchcraft works were published under my given name.

That wasn't because I didn't want readers of the occult works to know I was a Buddhist monk and abbot, or that I didn't want to Buddhist readers to know I was removed from my role as an Eastern Catholic archbishop-abbot because I am a Luciferian Witch.

It was simply because the proceeds of all of my books, classes and articles about Eastern mysticism and Buddhist philosophy were earmarked for the monastery, and our work feeding the homeless on the streets of Washington, D.C. and Atlanta, GA.

And so it's with considerable excitement that I've been able to turn the page, and unapologetically write and teach from the heart and mind, as a postmodern Witch, psychic intuitive, metaphysician and sojourner, who has no use for compartmentalization or filters.

That may become very evident in this book, which endeavours to bring together the wisdom of the East and West, in a volume dedicated to helping the reader uncover a technique used by Buddhist mystics, for centuries, to reclaim the mastery of one's mind; while drawing on the ancient insights of the Hermetic tradition of the West. It shouldn't be surprising for those two subjects to be covered in the same text, but it's apparently never been done until now.

Both of the source texts for this book, *Seven-Pointed Mind Training* (Wallace, 1992) from the Tibetan Buddhist tradition, and *The Kybalion* (Initiates, 1908), from the metaphysical/occult traditions, are recognized for their contributions to the societies out of which they arose. Each is something of a brief introduction to a once-secret mystical tradition, which has survived since antiquity. And both have garnered the attention of teachers in their respective fields, for decades.

So why try to turn this into something new? Why not publish two separate books, directed at the usual audiences for each source text?

The answer, for me at least, is that I write to share technology. A friend recently called me a "techno-witch", because he said I incorporate a lot of technology into my practice of the Craft, and I think he's right. So, both alchemy and the seven-pointed mind control approaches represent what could be called ancient technologies. Technology is defined as the collection of techniques, skills, methods, and processes used in the production of goods or services or in the accomplishment of objectives.

So, if one wishes to gain greater control over their mind – a common objective in both the practice of Buddhism and Hermeticism – then it would seem to be that this is as good a place as any to start.

I've found that it is in the everyday world, where we are most likely to encounter those people who frustrate, irritate and even intend to harm us most, that we can deepen our practice in ways that would take years longer, were we to simply sit on the cushion and meditate, or gaze into the flames of our coven's bonfire.

It's been my experience that one of the most effective tools to accomplish this is to use the *Lojong - Eight Verses on Mind Training* (Yenlak), and *Seven-Pointed Mind Training* written in 12th Century Tibet, by the monk Chekawa. Compiled in the fifteenth century, Mind Training: The Great Collection is the earliest anthology of a special genre of Tibetan literature known as *lojong* in Tibetan. The principal focus of these texts is the systematic cultivation of such altruistic thoughts and emotions as compassion, love, forbearance, and perseverance. The *lojong* (mind-training) teachings are highly revered by Buddhists for their pragmatism and down-to-earth advice on coping with the various challenges and hardships that unavoidably characterize everyday human existence.

Through the practice of *lojong*, we learn to connect with our world in an unconditionally constructive way and take full responsibility for our experiences. We learn to generate what is called "Relative Bodhicitta" — that is to say a compassionate heart — and with practice and realisation, aspire toward generating "Ultimate Bodhicitta" or the "open, mindful heart of Compassion and wisdom".

Similarly, one of the first texts I was given to study, as a young Witch, was a tattered copy of the *Kybalion*, which belonged to my great aunt, Irene Salvato. At its core, the aphorisms that provide the foundation for the text, which like the Seven-Pointed Mind Training text, claim to be from antiquity, attempt to unlock the signification and meaning of these apparently simple wisdom instructions, so that the reader may begin to harness the power of the mind itself.

It is my belief that it is not only possible but necessary for an *aggiornamento* – an opening of the windows of Tibetan Buddhism and Hermetic Alchemy to allow the fresh air of a postmodern ethos in, and to provide the space and potential for the essence of that path to be made more relevant, accessible and authentic for practitioners of holistic, pagan spirituality

The *Seven Points* discussed in the Tibetan text are actually something of a systematic and topical approach, which includes:

1. The Preliminary Practices
2. The Formal Practice
3. Using Adversity to Awaken
4. Life and Death
5. Benchmarks
6. Commitments
7. Guidelines

The text itself contains some fifty-seven proverbs, which originally served as a basis for a series of antidotes for the negative mental habits and ideations that cause us to suffer.

It is not my intention to translate these proverbs verbatim, but rather to provide a more culturally relevant and accessible interpretation of them, much as my *tsawa lama* (principal teacher) did for us.

Curiously, the Kybalion concentrates the vast body of teachings attributed to Hermes Trismegistus – a legendary, demi-god, who is said to have brought occult wisdom to the priests of Egypt in antiquity – into seven topical concepts as well:

1. Mentalism
2. Correspondence
3. Vibration
4. Polarity
5. Rhythm
6. Cause and Effect
7. Gender

I've chosen to present this material in three chapters. The first will be the presentation of the Tibetan texts, with commentary, in order to create a foundational basis for a daily practice of mind control. My experience has been that having this type of foundation makes it much easier for the practitioner to then apply the ancient Wisdom School teachings of the *Kybalion*, in a more meaningful and productive way; since it is only by first mastering the mind that the other principals of alchemy can be successfully employed.

I've enjoyed the privilege of learning these ancient Tibetan technologies from several of the most adept Buddhist masters of the modern era, and only after more than a decade and a half, felt like I was accomplished enough to translate the teachings into the postmodern vernacular in a way that is culturally relevant, while remaining faithful to the intent of the 12th Century Tibetan monk, Lama Chekawa.

Having had the great fortune of growing up in the rich hereditary tradition of Italian folk magick, known as *stregoneria*, my working with the text of the Kybalion has been deeply augmented by the oral tradition and Ways of my ancestors, whose magickal practice dates back to the fourth century Before the Common Era.

Therefore, it's my sincere wish that this short book inspires you, the reader, to leave behind any trepidation that might have prevented you from digging into these ancient texts and exploring the fundamentals of mind mastery in the 21st century.

Chapter One - Lojong

"Train impartially in every instance. Once deep and inclusive training has taken place, love everyone." These were the admonishments of the 5th Shamar Rinpoché, Könchok Yenlak (1526–83), in his presentation of the *lojong* (mind training) practice, based upon the aphorisms formulated in Tibet in the 12th century by Chekawa Yeshe Dorje.

In the simplest of terms, the practice of *lojong* involves refining and purifying one's motivations and attitudes. Developed over a 300-year period between 900 and 1200 CE, as part of the Mahāyāna school of Buddhism, by Atiśa Dīpaṃkara Śrījñāna (982–1054 CE), a Bengali meditation master.

Atiśa is said to have studied with Dharmakīrtiśrī in Sumatra for twelve years, before returning to India, but at an advanced age, accepted an invitation to teach in Tibet, where he stayed for the rest of his life.

The aphorisms on mind training in their present form were composed by Chekawa Yeshe Dorje (1101–1175 CE). According to one account, Chekhawa saw a text, written by Langri

Tangpa (1054–1123), laying on his cellmate's bed, open to the phrase: "Gain and victory to others, loss and defeat to oneself". The phrase struck him and upon discovering that Langri Tangpa was no longer alive, he studied instead with one of Tangpa's students, Sharawa Yönten Drak, for twelve years, after which time, he wrote the *Eight Verses for Training the Mind* (Tangpa, 2012)

The original text was arranged into seven sections and contained 59 separate aphorisms.

We would be remiss if not to mention, with great gratitude and affection the generous compassion and wisdom shared with us by the great Masters Cekawa, Kyabje Pabongkha Rinpoche, Kyabje Zong Rinpoche Dorje Chang, Kyabje Trijang Rinpoche Dorje Chang and Lama Thubten Yeshe, without whom we would not begin to comprehend this material.

Just as a lump of coal is transformed into a brilliant diamond, so too do their words of instruction transform these difficult and degenerate times into an opportunity for awakening.

THE PRELIMINARY PRACTICES

First, train in the preliminaries.

When we undertake the *Preliminary Practices* and start training our minds with the sayings of *Lojong* and *Tonglen*, we should always maintain a mindful awareness of the following key concepts, collectively referred to as "taking the attitude of the Four Reminders":

1.) **HUMAN BIRTH**: This human incarnation is precious, and we are fortunate to have been born in an environment in which we have the auspicious opportunity to hear the Dharma.

2.) **IMPERMANENCE**: Our lives are fragile and impermanent. Death is an inevitable reality and can come suddenly, and without warning.

3.) **THE DEFECTS OF SAMSARA**: In this samsaric existence, whatever you do, whether virtuous or not, only further ensnares you in the chain of cause and effect (karma).

4.) **THE REALITY OF SUFFERING**: You and all sentient beings inevitably and intensely experience suffering in this and all lives, while trapped in the cycle of samsara.

There is a tendency to imagine that this first point is unimportant because it is brief. Please don't allow yourself to suffer from that mistake. We could, in fact, spend days discussing each of these Four Reminders, but for the sake of brevity, this short booklet covers them in a more general way.

Jamgön Kongtrül Lodrö Thayé was a Tibetan Buddhist scholar, poet, artist, physician, tertön and metaphysician, and one of the most prominent Tibetan Buddhists of the 19th century. He is credited as one of the founders of the Rimé (non-sectarian) Buddhist movement, compiling what is known as the "Five Great Treasuries".

Speaking on the importance of the Preliminary Practices, Jamgon Kongtrul teaches, "You should energetically train yourself in this kind of thinking. At the end of every period of meditation, perform the seven-branch prayer as many times as you are able. In post-meditation periods, put the points of your reflections into practice."

THE MAIN PRACTICE

Consider all things and events as dreamlike.

Examine the nature of unborn awareness.

Let even the antidote be freed in its own place.

Rest in the ālaya, the essence.

Between sessions, be a conjurer of illusions.

The Second Point of Mind Training consists of nine focal points or key instructions. Originally, the texts called for training in what was called the "ultimate awakening mind", and then the "conventional awakening mind".

In this book, however, we have chosen to follow the example of our benevolent protector, Je Tsongkhapa, who reversed that order of training, in his work "*Mind Training like the Rays of the Sun*" (Pel, 1992).

And so first, we undertake the training in the conventional awakening mind:

Banish the one to blame for everything,

Meditate on the great kindness of all beings.

Practice a combination of giving and taking.

Giving and taking should be practised alternately

And you should begin by taking from yourself.

These two should be made to ride on the breath.

Concerning the three objects, three poisons and three virtues,

The instruction to be followed, in short,

Is to be mindful of the practice in general,

By taking these words to heart in all activities.

BANISHING THE NEED TO BLAME OTHERS

On the Formal Practice, Chögyam Trungpa Rinpoche writes:

You can experience that dreamlike quality by relating to sitting meditation practice. When you are reflecting on the breath, suddenly discursive thoughts begin to arise; you begin to see things, to hear things, and to feel things. But all those perceptions are none other than your own mental creation. In the same way, you can see that your hate for your enemy, your love for your friends, and your attitude toward money, food, and wealth are all part of discursive thought. (Rinpoche C. T., 1981)

In Buddhism, we recognise that this aggregate of systems and senses we imagine as our "self" is merely an illusion. One of the principal benefits of this practice is that it restores a sort of gentleness... a soft, comforting reminder of what our True Nature, which is Consciousness, or *Śunyata*, or Love, or God(dess), etc., already knows. It's about the process of rediscovering truths that we already possess, which might have been obscured by the dreamlike state.

Everything that appears in your experience is a manifestation of your mind. And it is also a reflection of something within you that needs your attention.

While we dream, the events in our dreams seem really to be happening we find ourselves in another location, conversations take place, we experience pain or pleasure, fear or calm. Anything can happen in your dreams. All the appearances are there. But despite these appearances, no such events have really occurred while you slept. And so, it is with what we imagine to be our "waking state", which is but another level of dream-consciousness.

The first instruction is very simple, yet profound. We should not lay the blame for anything on others.

Now, as simple as it sounds, I know that there will be, for many of my readers, a momentary rolling of the eyes, because this sounds rather absurd on the surface. After all, if someone attacks us on the street, why would we not say that they were to blame?

You see, all our attackers would have provided, would be the momentary circumstance for injury to occur. This returns to what we call **100% responsibility.**

We must recognise that every experience begins in our minds. And if that is true, and if our perception of this "self", which is really nothing more than an aggregate of senses and systems, then it is also true that we are responsible for bringing forth the misery in samsara from the beginning was time. To the degree that we continue this self-cherishing, the self-cleaning attitude we will experience suffering and harm in this lifetime.

Now it's also very important, to understand that we don't mean instead of blaming other people, we blame ourselves. Our objective is to take a closer look at what blame feels like altogether, and then to guard ourselves against the temptation to engage in that hurtful, meaningless, and immature practice.

When you really think about it, it takes so much energy to place blame. I believe that most occurrences of placing blame have their roots in fear. When we are afraid that someone is taking something from us, doing something that will hurt us, making us look less important, less honourable, less "good", then the ego self, begins the process of pointing fingers.

The very moment that we begin to take 100% responsibility, when we begin to say, "I have chosen this experience, these are the seeds I planted, and now I am reaping the crop at harvest time," everything changes. When we realise that the ordinary mind throws the responsibility on someone else and that the perception of the other is an illusion, we return to the point of power within ourselves. Pure Awareness.

I like to end this section of the commentary by sharing something Albert Einstein wrote, which might have just as easily been written by a great Dharma master:

A human being is a part of the whole, called by us, "Universe," a part limited in time and space. He experiences himself, his thoughts and feelings as something separated from the rest — a kind of optical delusion of his consciousness.

This delusion is a kind of prison for us, restricting us to our personal desires and to affection for a few persons nearest to us. Our task must be to free ourselves from this prison by widening our circle of compassion to embrace all living creatures and the whole of nature in its beauty.

Nobody can achieve this completely, but the striving for such achievement is in itself a part of the liberation and a foundation for inner security.

Nothing exists independently of consciousness or mental designation.

CULTIVATING GRATITUDE FOR ALL SENTIENT BEINGS

The respected Buddhist teacher, Ani Pema Chodron reminds us that the slogan "be grateful to everyone" is about making peace with all of the aspects of ourselves that we may

What exactly does that mean? How do we allow our practice of *tonglen* to ride the waves of our breath?

The practice of *tonglen* is a very important part of my personal practice and was considered by our lineage masters to be of great importance for every practitioner. In fact, the great master Shantideva said,

Whoever wishes quickly to become a refuge for himself and others, should undertake this sacred mystery: to take the place of others, giving them his own.

Tonglen is the practice of open-hearted generosity and compassion.

The word *tonglen* literally means "giving and taking," and is a spiritual, mind-training exercise, in which one mentally gives up one's peace, in exchange for the suffering of another. It is not that we imagine that we literally possess the ability to do so, but the practice directs the mind toward healing and generates genuine compassion. From the cultivation of this genuine compassion, one learns to generate the "Mind of Enlightenment", Bodhicitta.

Ani Pema Chodron teaches that doing tonglen "sweeps away the dust that has been covering over your treasure that's always been there," — we call this the Bodhicitta Heart.

In the *Eight Verses of Mind Training* (Lojong), we are told to practice *tonglen* by "secretly taking on the suffering of others". One does not announce to the person for whom they are engaging this practice that they will be taking on their suffering.

Tonglen can be practised any time you perceive that a negative situation has arisen. Breathing in, you imagine yourself taking in the negativity, and breathing out, you send forth love-kindness, peace, calm and joy. The practice of *tonglen* neutralizes the dualistic tendencies of the mind, by refocusing on the true nature, which is Compassion.

When one commits to practising *tonglen*, they move beyond the self-absorption that lives in a sea of excuses and imagine that there are more important things to do. They move beyond fear and suspicion of others, and in fact, move beyond the illusion of "otherness" altogether.

Now, because there are countless beings in our experience of the cosmos, it would be unwise to try to give your happiness to *all beings* right off the bat! You might not have time for anything else!

The great teachers all recommend that you begin by visualizing in front of you, someone you dearly love — your mother perhaps.

Reflect on how she suffered the pains of carrying you and giving you birth. Call to mind the difficulty she must have had walked, getting up from a seated position, perhaps holding down food in the morning, just so that you could have this precious birth.

Next, as you inhale, feel yourself taking on any suffering your mother has endured, and as you breathe out, send love, peace and comfort. Do this for ten or fifteen minutes, feeling each time that your mother begins to smile a little more, and becomes lighter in her being and countenance.

Then, imagine that deep within you, at the base of your spine is a furnace, like the old-fashioned coal burning or wood-burning stoves. This furnace is the furnace of Kundalini, and into it, you can place all the negativity, suffering and darkness you took on from your mother, and use it as fuel so that nothing negative remains.

The next time you sit to practice, you will do the same thing, but expand your desire to alleviate your mother's suffering by recognising that all beings have, at one time or other, being your mother. And thus you can expand your practice of taking and giving to include your family, your friends, your community, etc., each time expanding another level, until you truly begin to feel yourself taking in the suffering of all sentient beings and using it as fuel, as you send out love, compassion, gentle healing and peace.

See yourself breathing in heavy, oppressive, ominous negativity and suffering, and as the fire of Kundalini burns it as fuel, you send out a brilliant white, luminous light, that's calm and healing.

What does this practice of *tonglen* accomplish?

Generally speaking, happiness & suffering occur as a result of karma – the interdependent chain of conditions/causes and their effects. If someone has done a good action, then naturally from that there will come a result of happiness. That result of happiness that cannot be denied the practitioner, because it is simply the result of the causes they created.

Likewise, suffering occurs as a result of bad actions. If someone has acted in a way that is not healthy, useful or meritorious, then the only result that can be obtained from that is suffering. This is not a punitive situation, but rather the natural response of universal law, much like gravity.

It's important to realise that this practice is not something that necessarily brings some type of literal relief for those who suffer. One should not, for example, become disheartened when doing *tonglen* for a loved one, who is seriously ill, if that person continues to suffer and become more ill. The point of the practice is not some sort of new age hocus-pocus, but again to plant the seeds (causes) for relief of suffering.

Perhaps it seems at this moment you are not able to bring happiness or remove suffering, but by doing this practice will help you gradually cease to cherish yourself over others. You will instead develop the wish to practice in order to benefit other beings, eventually leading to the ability to help beings, teach and train them in the Dharma, and so forth.

Consequently, one will be able to give them happiness and relieve them of suffering and offer them whatever qualities and abilities that one has.

This is called *relative bodhicitta*.

The other form of bodhicitta, *ultimate bodhicitta*, is approached by pacifying concepts and dualism: all one's thoughts are calmed; one's clinging to dualism assuaged; one just rests in the state of peace, of meditation. One dissolves into emptiness and just rests in the true nature of the mind.

By engaging in the *tonglen* practice, you create the causes to attain the state of ultimate bodhicitta. As Yoda tells us, in The Empire Strikes Back, "Always in motion is the future..." Likewise, always in motion, we could say, is the past.

The reason for this is that the greater the compassion and awareness we generate, the clearer our perceptions become, and those things we once feared, or resented, or clung to gradually slip into emptiness, freeing us to become Pure Love.

Ani Pema Chodron reminds us:

What you do for yourself – any gesture of kindness, any gesture of gentleness, any gesture of honesty and clear seeing toward yourself – will affect how you experience your world. In fact, it will transform how you experience the world. What you do for yourself, you're doing for others, and what you do for others, you're doing for yourself. When you exchange self for others in the practice of tonglen, it becomes increasingly uncertain what is out there and what is in here.

And so, we are ready to begin looking at the real cultivation of Bodhicitta.

Śantidev tells us that we always have a choice in how we approach life's challenges:

If the road is covered with rocks and thorns,

you can either pave the entire road with leather,

or you can take a piece of leather

and place it on the soles of your own feet.

This section concludes with the instruction, *"Understand the Three Objects, Three Poisons, Three Virtues."*

Here, what Atiśa refers to are the three objects of inner alchemy, which can either become aversions (poisons) or the foundations of infinite virtues.

WHAT ARE THESE THREE OBJECTS?

The first is an aversion, the second is attachment, and the third is indifference. This is how the mind functions. You feel aversion to whatsoever you dislike, you feel an attachment to whatever you like, and you feel indifferent to things which you neither dislike nor like.

When we encounter people, objects or situations which please us, we experience attachment. However, when those same people, objects or situations cause us to be uncomfortable, or we perceive them as people or things we don't like or consider our "enemies", we experience aversion.

His Holiness Dilgo Khyentse Rinpoche explains it this way: "In pleasant situations, we feel attachment; in unpleasant situations, anger; in indifferent situations, ignorance."

Atiśa knew these three poisons, which so many of us are prone to, can become the bases of virtue if we mindfully generate compassion. Here is what he said about this:

If you learn the art of absorbing suffering as if all the suffering of the world is coming riding on the breath, then how can you be repulsed? How can you dislike anything and how can you be indifferent to anything?

If you are unconditionally taking in all the suffering of the world, drinking it, absorbing it into your heart, and then instead of it pouring blessings on the whole of existence – UNCONDITIONALLY; not to someone in particular, remember; not only to man but to all; to all beings, trees and rocks and birds and animals, to the whole existence – material, immaterial – when you are pouring out blessings unconditionally, how can you be attached?

This simple exercise can have profound implications in your life and in the lives of those you encounter.

We need only train ourselves to think, moment by moment:

May the obscurations of all beings, arising through these three poisons, come upon me like a load to bear. May all beings live virtuously, performing positive actions, and be free from the three poisons of attachment, anger and ignorance.

Attachment, aversion, indifference; all disappear with this small technique. And with their disappearance the poison is transformed into nectar, and the bondage becomes freedom, and the hell is no more hell, it is heaven.

IN ALL WE DO...

The next instruction in the Seven-Pointed Mind Training tells us: "Apply these proverbs in all that you do."

The idea is that we should allow these maxims and proverbs to become anchor points in our minds, to help us cultivate the right attitudes and discipline.

For me, one of the most profound maxims, which captures the Mystic Heart perfectly comes from Śantideva: "While their negative karma ripens in me, let my virtuous karma ripen in them."

The Kadam tradition interprets this idea a little differently, saying: "I offer all gain and victory to all sentient beings, and take all loss and defeat for myself."

That particular way of expressing that maxim is one of those culturally dissonant ideas, which would seem very emotionally and psychologically unhealthy for those of us in the West. For that reason, I don't particularly use it.

The idea, however, is that we are taking on the suffering of others and sending out the victory and joy that is within us. Doing so doesn't really mean we give away our joy, because true joy can never be depleted. It is simply a matter of adopting the right attitude of selflessness toward "others". In time, we would let go of such an attitude, because we would recognise that there is no "other" nor is there a "self".

But these are gradual steps, and as such we begin with the idea of *tonglen* – taking and receiving. Our actual attitude, whether we rely on the maxim by Śantidev or the Kadampa version, is that we are sincerely asking the Universal Consciousness, "May the suffering of all sentient beings be drawn to my own self-grasping mind, so that it might be vanquished entirely."

The Zen master Sechibuwa offers another potent maxim, with a more positive approach: "By my joy, may all sentient beings experience joy."

Our experiences are formed in our minds and are inherently empty. Therefore, why not use the mind to cultivate joy and equanimity?

As the Tao reminds us, "We shape clay into a pot, but it is the emptiness inside that holds whatever we want."

Transforming Adversity into the Path of Enlightenment

When all the world is filled with evil,

transform adversity into the path of enlightenment.

Drive all blames into one.

Meditate on the great kindness of all.

Meditating on delusory perceptions as the four kāyas.

Is the unsurpassable śūnyatā protection.

The fourfold practice is the best of methods.

Whatever you encounter, apply the practice.

In the next section of the text, we find the following instructions:

When stability has been attained, impart the secret teaching:

- *Consider all phenomena as being like dreams,*

- *Examine the nature of unborn awareness.*

- *The remedy itself is released in its own place,*

- *Place the essence of the path on the nature of the basis of all.*

- *In the period between sessions, be a creator of illusions.*

CONSIDER ALL PHENOMENA AS DREAMS

This next instruction has been one which, for me personally, has been one of the most powerfully transformative keys to surviving and thriving in the face of seeming adversity.

It's about learning to recognise that at any given moment, our idea of reality is being interpreted through the cloudy, muddled lens of our dualistic perceptions, our fears, and chaotic data, stored on the hard drive of our subconscious minds.

Think for a moment about someone you dislike a great deal. In your mind, you've probably created an idea that this person will be permanently bad, or distasteful or even evil. Am I right?

As a result, your every interaction with that person is coloured by that perception. There was a man from the Karma Kagyu sect of Tibetan Buddhism, who at one time, was quite the celebrity on the Buddhist and Yoga blogging scene. As his ego began to get bigger than the Karma Kagyu sect itself, he soon began to seemingly act out in mean-spirited, argumentative and downright nasty ways.

Eventually, he began to attack me, because I refused to partake in a sickening witch-hunt that he had undertaken in his effort to purge the Americas of unorthodox Buddhist teachers. Later, he would realise the very reason for that was not only that I happened to personally like and respect the two teachers he was attacking, but that I too am an unorthodox teacher, to be certain.

In my mind, I had decided this was a hateful, arrogant and disgusting little troll of a man, right down to his Ziggy Top beard, and hillbilly overalls.

And then, in a rare moment of lucidity, I began to look at this man for what he was -- a reflection of something within me that needed to be corrected.

Suddenly, I realised that he was suffering from a great deal of anger over health issues that were robbing him of his vibrancy and mobility. I could understand that, as someone living with AIDS and Parkinson's Disease for the past twenty-some years.

And do you know what? Within days, the daily attacks on Twitter and Facebook just ended... after three years of constant badgering, back-biting and attempt to discredit me.

This man, who succeeded in personally scaring off every one of our financial benefactors, and who had forced us into a position where we only ate every other day, because otherwise, we could not afford to keep the lights on in our hermitage... who forced us to live through 14-20 degree weather, with the heat in the hermitage set no higher than 47 degrees, because we could not afford the oil bill... suddenly, and without explanation, stopped attacking us.

You see, while we slept, the dream seemed quite real... but the moment we awaken from the dream, we realise that wasn't so. These appearances, which make up our everyday experience, are simply our mind's manifestations of confusion.

Dreams sometimes appear to be totally realistic and have the ability to cause our pulse to race, our bodies to sweat and shake... even though they are not anything more than our thoughts. In the same way, we can train our minds to recognise that those experiences that play out in our 'waking dreams' are simply the result of our thoughts... illusions deeply rooted in our subconscious minds.

Viewing each phenomenon as existing by itself, completely independent of its surroundings, causes, conditions, and our mental labelling of it, is the same as regarding dreams as real. By learning to see every experience as a dream - whether good or bad - we organically lose our attachment to them. We relax into the moment and allow Pure Awareness to arise within us.

EXAMINE THE NATURE OF UNBORN AWARENESS

As we "examine the nature of unborn awareness", I think one of the most beautiful explanations comes from Ani Pema Chodron's book, *"Start Where You Are: A Guide to Compassionate Living"*, in which she explains:

> *When we awaken our hearts, we're changing the whole pattern, but not by creating a new pattern. We are moving further and further away from concretizing and making things so solid and always trying to get some ground underneath our feet. This moving away from comfort and security, this stepping out into the unknown, uncharted, and shaky – that's called enlightenment, liberation.* (Chodron, 1994)

So, this maxim is really about learning to look at our raw, undivided mind, with pure awareness. Examining "who" is this "me" that is thinking. In other words, it pulls the rug out from under you, in case the previous maxim made you feel like "you" had accomplished something!

Far too often, we focus our meditation on objects. What are we mindful of? Where is our attention in that situation? On the object itself... the "what". And since we know that all phenomena are impermanent, focusing on something impermanent will never yield useful results.

This maxim encourages us to shift our awareness from what we are mindful of, to WHY we are mindful. And that is altogether different, isn't it? It requires deep digging, and we will ultimately realise there is no substantial reason. And so, as we realise that these thoughts are without rational reason, then pure awareness allows everything else upon which we've focused to dissolve... we begin to exist in the realm of Pure Awareness. Not thinking. Not focusing. Simply being Pure Awareness. And that is what this maxim is designed to do.

LET GO OF EVERYTHING, INCLUDING THE REMEDY ITSELF

The next maxim instructs: *In time, even let go of everything, including the remedy itself...*

As our spiritual practice and meditative focus turns to outer phenomena, we will begin to understand the inherent emptiness of all phenomena. But emptiness does not exist by itself. For example, we can contemplate this web page, which does not exist independently but is the result (demonstration) of dependent origination. Therefore, we can say that the essential nature of this webpage is emptiness. However, without this object-base (the webpage), even emptiness does not independently exist.

As it is said in the *Heart of Wisdom Discourse*:

> 0 Sariputra, form here is emptiness and emptiness indeed is form. Emptiness is not different from form; form is not different from emptiness. What is form, that is emptiness; what is emptiness, that is form. The same applies to feeling, recognition, karmic formations, and consciousness...

In other words, this point in the *Formal Practice* tells us that we cannot substitute one belief system for another. We must eventually let go of our beliefs altogether.

This is called *"resting in the nature of Alaya"* (which we'll get to in a moment). And I would suggest it is one of the things most sorely needed in the practice of many spiritual groups, especially Tibetan Buddhists and Pagans. They become so wrapped up in what is and is not "authentic" Tibetan Buddhism (or Witchcraft, or Tarot Divination, or Hoodoo, etc.)

Their pocket-books get threatened by anything that might cause someone to stop sending them all their money, and so they write absurd suggestions, such as the recent suggestion that exploring new ways of making ancient spiritual traditions more relevant and accessible somehow threatens them and "ruins it for everyone else". In short, they're simply demonstrating how little progress they've made and how poorly they understand the Universal Law.

The beloved master, His Holiness Dilgo Khyentse Rinpoche, once wrote:

> *People who ask for Dharma teachings do so because they are afraid of what might happen to them after death. They decide that they must take refuge, request the lama for instruction and concentrate unwaveringly on the practice: a hundred thousand prostrations, a hundred thousand mandala offerings, recitations of the refuge formula and so on.*
>
> *These, of course, are positive thoughts, but thoughts, being without substantial nature, do not stay for very long. When the teacher is no longer present and there is no one to show*

what should and should not be done, then for most practitioners it is as the saying goes: Old yogis getting rich; old teachers getting married. This only goes to show that thoughts are impermanent, and we should, therefore, bear in mind that any thought or antidote – even the thought of emptiness is itself by nature empty without substantial existence. (Rinpoche D. K., 1993)

So, go ahead... pull the rug out from under your beliefs. In the end, it doesn't make a bit of difference whether it's Buddhism, Christianity, Shintoism, Wiccan, Norse Paganism, Witchcraft, Voodoo or Islam... we need to go beyond that antidote.

APPLYING THE PRACTICE THROUGHOUT THE WHOLE OF LIFE

The essence of the instruction briefly stated,

is to apply yourself to the five strengths.

The mahāyāna advice for transference

Involves the same five strengths. Conduct is important.

Our next maxim in the *Formal Practice* admonishes us to "rest our minds in their natural state — *alaya* — which is a word representing the open primordial basis of all phenomena.

In essence, this instruction is something of a culmination of the previous ones, because it's about realising the true nature of all phenomena (emptiness) and letting go of our delusional notions of things existing independently. Therefore, by sustaining and allowing our minds to rest in this pure awareness, we allow the space for our understanding to become transformed.

As our understanding is transformed, deeper realisations are able to occur. In time, this will dissipate the weaker energy of ignorance, and we will be able to maintain this pure, meditative equipoise in all our activities — even when we leave the mat/cushion.

One beloved student once said that it was difficult for him to accept my recommendation that we simply ignore those who have made a career of attacking and disparaging our teaching. "Where is the justice in that?" they understandably asked in frustration.

When we perceive an attacker, our reaction to them is always based on the false perception that their attack is real, true and permanent reality. In fact, it is nothing at all. For this reason, we can rest our minds in the *Alaya Nature* — the mind beyond all elaborations, and beyond all concepts, and know that we are safe and secure because one cannot attack emptiness itself, especially with something that isn't real.

It has been said that if awareness needs a method it is still not true awareness, but rather a byproduct of the dualistic mind. Right now, when we dwell deeply in the present moment, there is nothing to do. Only this moment exists. And when you begin to dwell deeply in this moment, there is pure awareness, with no effort, with no method... just resting in the nature of Alaya.

In his book, "*The Great Path of Awakening: An Easily Accessible Introduction for Ordinary People*", Jamgon Kongtrul Rinpoche teaches:

> "*When you look directly at the presence of mind, no colour, no shape, no form is perceived. Since mind has no origin, it has never come into existence in the first place. Now it is not located anywhere, inside or outside the body. Finally, the mind is not some object that goes somewhere or ceases to exist. By examining and investigating mind, you should come to a precise and certain understanding of the nature of this awareness, which has no origin, location, or cessation.*"
> (Rinpoche J. K., 1987)

THE MEASURE OF MIND TRAINING

All teachings share a single purpose.

Of the two witnesses, rely upon the principal one.

Always maintain only a joyful attitude.

If this can be done even when distracted, you are proficient.

The fifth maxim tells us to remain mindful that we are a "child of illusion", even when we are no longer "actively" meditating. In other words, we continue to engender an awareness that all appearances, including what we think of as ourselves are ultimately illusions.

I think that Ani Pema Chodron again puts it most succinctly in, *"Start Where You Are: A Guide to Compassionate Living"* when she writes:

> *Being a child of illusion also has to do with beginning to encourage yourself not to be a walking battleground...the truth is that good and bad coexist; sour and sweet coexist. They aren't really opposed to each other...The Buddha within is messy as well as clean.*

We generally interpret the world so heavily in terms of good and bad, happy and sad, nice and not nice, that the world doesn't have a chance to speak for itself. When we say, "Be a child of illusion," we're beginning to get at this fresh way of looking where we're not caught up in our hope and fear. (Chodron, 1994)

Now, this isn't an encouragement to try our hand at walking through walls or setting ourselves on fire. This world we created is very real in our minds. What we are doing in this practice is cultivating mindfulness that sees beyond the limitations, illusions and notions we've constructed, and recognises the potential for peace and calm in every moment.

By working with the practice of *Lojong*, we can develop better control over our emotional states, and bring about what we refer to as "calm abiding" — the state in which we are able to more effectively use our minds, rather than having our minds use us. There is no need to control the mind which has been cultivated and trained.

We imagine that this state of being, this aggregate of senses and systems we call the body is the ultimate state for expressing life. But when we begin to cultivate a still, peaceful and calm mind, we begin to realise there is something beyond this frenetic state of being — a state of pure awareness that lies beyond the limitations of space and time.

THE COMMITMENTS OF MIND TRAINING

Train constantly in three basic principles.

Change your attitude but remain natural.

Don't speak of injured limbs.

Don't ponder others' flaws.

Train first with the strongest destructive emotions.

Abandon any expectations of results.

Give up poisonous food.

Don't be so loyal to the cause.

Don't lash out in retaliation.

Don't lie in ambush.

Don't strike a vulnerable point.

Don't transfer the ox's burden to the cow.

Don't be competitive.

Don't perform the rites improperly.

Don't reduce gods to demons.

Don't seek others' misery as crutches of your own happiness.

Next, the instruction tells us how to transform adverse conditions and circumstances into the Path to Enlightenment. The text reads:

When the environment and its inhabitants overflow with unwholesomeness,

Transform adverse circumstances into the path to enlightenment.

Apply meditation immediately at every opportunity.

The supreme method is accompanied by the Five Practices.

This set of maxims is really a series focused on expanding our awareness and capacity for abundance. Again, realising that we create our experiences as a mirror-reflection of the condition of our minds, we find ourselves often trapped in a self-created poverty mentality. This sense of poverty does not only concern itself with finances, but with the quality of relationships, opportunities, and interactions in our lives.

In short, it's the "poor me" pity party, which creates all of these adverse circumstances.

And so, we undertake the task of learning to see everything that occurs, both serene and chaotic, as opportunities for us to awaken.

This is why we practice *tonglen* so that we can strengthen that awareness that the very reason we see others suffering, is because we too have suffered. The person who has treated us harshly is mirroring the times when we have treated others harshly.

Therefore, since we have been angry, depressed, frightened, or alone, we are able to exchange ourselves for others, realising that they are precious gifts in our lives, and deserve to find the peace that is their inherent nature; for they have been serving as teachers for us. If we are not grateful for each of these teachers, then we will have to repeat the lesson, again and again, until we learn to be grateful.

Here, I think the sage observations of His Holiness Dilgo Khyentse Rinpoche speak more clearly about this than I could ever hope to do:

All suffering comes through not recognizing ego-clinging as our enemy. When we are hit by a stick or a stone, it hurts; when someone calls us a thief or a liar, we become angry. Why is this? It is because we feel great esteem and attachment for what we think of as our selves, and we think, 'I am being attacked.' Clinging to the 'I' is the real obstacle to the attainment of liberation and enlightenment.

What we call obstacle-makers or evil influences, such as ghosts, gods, and so on, are not at all entities outside us. It is from within that the trouble comes. It is due to our fixation on 'I' that we think: 'I am so unhappy, I can't get anything to eat, I have no clothes, lots of people are against me and I don't have any friends.' It is thoughts like these that keep us so busy - and all so uselessly.

This is the reason why we are not on the path to liberation and Buddhahood. Throughout the entire succession of our lives, from beginningless time until the present, we have been taking birth in one or another of the six realms. How long have we been labouring in the three worlds of samsara, slaves to our ego-clinging! This is why we cannot escape. When a man has borrowed a lot of money, he will never have a moment's peace until he has repaid his debt.

So it is with all the work that our ego-clinging has given us to do; it has left negative imprints on the alaya similar to promissory notes. When our karma fructifies and 'payment' is demanded, we have no chance for happiness and enjoyment. All this is because, as it says in the teachings, we do not recognise ego-clinging as our real enemy. (Rinpoche D. K., 1993)

Hand in hand with that first maxim, in this section, we find that the more aware we become of this, the more comfortable and relaxed we become in our lives. As a result, we don't react to circumstances and situations. We don't feel "victimised" by everything. And so, we are able to begin to treat these unexpected occurrences with an attitude of meditative awareness.

Let me share an example. I was recently asked to partner with someone who wanted to teach a series of workshops on the path of forgiveness and mind training. Unfortunately, this individual, while sincerely interested in helping others alleviate suffering in their lives, has not got the formal training or understanding of these principles, and as such, has never applied them to his own life fully.

When I made the mistake of ghost-writing a book for this person, to help get the process underway, I assumed he would read the book I wrote, and begin to apply those principles to his life, so that he would have the more important benefit of experience as his teacher. But what happened was that he became anxious and perhaps a little concerned that I was very relaxed and clear about the material, and he didn't want to appear to be contradicting himself or unsure, not only from an ego perspective but genuinely out of concern for those taking the workshop.

He began to look to many other approaches, trying to synthesise a number of New Age ideas, which focus on other people's "magical" or "metaphysical" skills, being necessary to achieve healing... looking outside of himself... and contradicting the simplicity and efficacy of this path. And the more he did that, the more agitated he was becoming by my Dharma talks.

Now, let's remember, I had been teaching this material for 29 years, by this point... essentially saying the same thing that entire time. But suddenly, he was taking everything as a confrontation, because he was contradicting the ancient wisdom of these traditions with his *latest* tangential belief.

This man began to have a meltdown, and finally blurted out what I had known about him for decades -- that he had no respect for me, resented my natural leadership abilities, perceiving them as a need to "control" him, and that he was incapable of seeing the historic and philosophical interconnectivity of the various components of the path we were to teach, because he was not yet at a place in his life where letting go of duality was even possible.

Immediately, I thought about the story of the man coming to spit in Buddha's face. I didn't get worked up over it. I simply used it as a meditation. And I shared with him that I was glad he finally let all those things -- those poisons, which destroyed every project the two of us ever attempted in the past -- to come to the surface and be released.

Now, the testimony to this man's genuine compassion and sincerity came as he took time to "clean" on the very situation himself, and taking 100% Responsibility, realised none of this was about what it appeared to be. And I believe that the first steps toward letting go of his resentment for me began that day. But more importantly, we resolved that karma, which had kept us bound to one another and to failure, so that we could then move on toward the next step in our Paths to Enlightenment.

As Dilgo Khyentse Rinpoche tells us, whenever these difficulties arise, we should think: If we are struck by evil forces, we should think, *"By making me suffer, these evil beings are helping me to practice Bodhicitta; they are of great importance for my progress on the path, and rather than being expelled, they should be thanked."*

We should be as grateful to them as we are towards our teachers.

THE FIVE PRACTICES

We are finally told that in order to synthesise the essence of this teaching, we should rely on the Five Practices:

- The Practice of Resolution

- The Practice of Familiarisation

- The Practice of Cultivating the Seed of Virtue

- The Practice of Reproach

- The Practice of Aspiration

So, let's unpack these, one at a time:

1. The Practice of Resolution - This is a reliance on a determined resolve not to become distracted from cultivating relative and ultimate Bodhicitta. It is a commitment to remain steadfast until we realise our Awakened Mind, for the sake of all sentient beings. Ani Pema Chodron reminds us that this type of determination is relaxed, joyful and trusting. It isn't forced or drudgery.

2. The Practice of Familiarisation - When we begin to truly embrace the Dharma, then it no longer feels like "an ancient Eastern approach" or a foreign way of thinking. It becomes our way of thinking until every thought you think becomes instruction in the Dharma itself. We recognise that the most efficient way for this to occur is to engage in consistent practice so that we familiarise ourselves with the dharmic way of seeing and responding to the actions of the mind. The more familiar we become... the more natural this way of life begins to transform us... the greater the opportunity for spiritual breakthroughs, and cultivation of wisdom, compassion and loving-kindness.

3. The Practice of Virtue - Imagine that your spiritual practice is a precious seed, from which the great tree of Virtue will grow. Once you've planted that seed, your responsibility isn't over. You must nurture the seed until it matures into its ultimate potential. It is also a reminder that we need not keep searching elsewhere, but diligently provide the moisture, warmth and light needed, so that the first sprouts of that tree of virtue eventually emerge from the fertile soil of our practice, where they will continue to be nurtured to full realisation.

4. The Practice of Reproach - This is the practice of committing ourselves to catch our minds the moment before we do anything to create the causes for further samsara, and to break our self-cherishing, attachments and aversions on the spot. Recognising that it is our self-centred ego mind that obstructs us from realisation, we mindfully choose not to succumb to its interference in our practice.

5. The Practice of Aspiration - Whenever we have completed some positive action we should make the following prayer of aspiration, "From now on until I attain enlightenment, may I never abandon the two Bodhicittas. Whatever conflicts I may encounter, may I be able to use them as steps along the path."

This is not a prayer in the sense of asking some supernatural being to bestow some gift upon you, but rather a declarative statement to your True Nature, that seals your commitment to the Bodhisattva Path.

It is this resolve and aspiration which will allow you to be relaxed and joyful in your practice because you will know that in this very moment, you have done all you can to accomplish realisation. No stressing about the future, no guilt about the past. You are simply dwelling deeply in the Pure Awareness that is the present moment.

THE PRECEPTS OF MIND TRAINING

Do everything with a single intention.

Counter all adversity with a single remedy.

Two tasks: one at the beginning and one at the end.

Whichever of the two occurs, be patient.

Keep the two, even at your life's expense.

Train in the three difficulties.

Acquire the three main provisions.

Cultivate the three that must not decline.

Keep the three from which you must not separate.

Apply the training impartially to all.

It is vital that it be deep and all-pervasive.

Meditate constantly on those who've been set apart.

Don't be dependent on external conditions.

This time, practise what's most important.

Don't misunderstand.

Don't be inconsistent.

Train wholeheartedly.

Gain freedom through discernment and analysis.

Don't be boastful.

Don't be irritable.

Don't be temperamental.

Don't seek acknowledgement.

The Measure of Having Trained the Mind

So begins the next maxim:

Integrate all the teachings into one thought,

Primary importance should be given to the two witnesses,

Constantly cultivate only a peaceful mind.

The measure of a trained mind is that it has turned away,

There are five great marks of a trained mind.

The trained (mind) retains control even when distracted.

Cultivate these paths of practice.

As a practitioner, it is likely that you have encountered a varied array of spiritual approaches, practices and sadhanas, influenced by your particular path. These might include ritual invocation, pranayama, mindfulness practice, *Metta*, candle magick, *Lam Rim Chenmo*, meditation on emptiness, and so forth. The single purpose of these practices is to assist you in letting go.

In fact, it can be said that the entire objective of all of the Buddha's 84,000 teachings, all of the commentaries by the great masters, and every tradition that arose from the original schools of Dharma, is to eliminate self-grasping, self-cherishing and the attempt to avoid pain. In other words -- shedding the ego-mind.

I like the way that Ani Pema Chodron explains the ego. She writes:

> *Ego is like a room of your own, a room with a view, with the temperature and the smells and the music that you like. You want it your way. You'd like to have a little peace: you'd lie to have a little happiness, you know, just "gimme a break!"*

> *But the more you think that way, the more you try to get life to come out so that it will always suit you, the more your fear of other people and what's outside your room grows. Rather than becoming more relaxed, you start pulling down the shades and locking the door. You become touchier, more fearful, more irritable than ever. The more you just try to get it your way, the less you feel at home.*

> *To begin to develop compassion for yourself and others, you have to unlock the door. You don't open it yet, because you have to work with your fear that somebody you don't like*

might come in. Then as you begin to relax and befriend those feelings, you begin to open it.

Sure enough, in come the music and the smells that you don't like. Sure enough, someone puts a foot in and tells you that you should have a different religion or vote for someone you don't like or give money that you don't want to give. Now you begin to relate to those feelings. You develop some compassion, connecting with the soft spot.

...When you begin to practice in this way, you're so honest about what you're feeling that it begins to create a feeling of understanding other people as well... We become part of a people who have cultivated their bravery throughout history, people who, against enormous odds, have stayed open to great difficulties and painful situations and transformed them into the path of awakening. We WILL fall flat on our faces, again and again, we WILL continue to feel inadequate, and we can use these experiences to wake up, just as they did. The lojong teachings give us the means to connect with the power of our lineage, the lineage of gentle warriorship. (Chodron, 1994)

Therefore, the essence of this maxim is to help you recognise that the extent to which you overcome your self-attachment; you will have begun to integrate the Dharma into your life.

UNDERSTANDING THE TWO WITNESSES

In any given situation, there are always what we call "*two witnesses*", or as I prefer, "two perspectives": the perspective others have of you, and your own perspective of yourself.

Your principal witness is always your own insight. What others think of you is irrelevant and none of your business.

Instead, start watching your thoughts, desires, dreams, motivations and agendas. Create a new kind of awareness within yourself. Become a Silent Centre, which goes on watching whatever is happening. You are angry, and you watch it. Suddenly, you are no longer just angry... a new element has been introduced into the equation: you are watching it. And the miracle is that if you can watch that anger, the anger disappears without being repressed.

We call this witnessing the witness itself.

SUSTAIN YOURSELF BY INNER HAPPINESS

One of the great benefits to the Kadampa Mind Training is that it sharpens and shifts our perspective, so that regardless of the seeming adversity at the moment, we can remain truly peaceful and joyful. Why? Because this training allows us to recognise the power and strength of our own mind.

It's about taking 100% responsibility and knowing that we are the creators of our experiences.

Not long ago, I made a terrible error in judgment, by agreeing to ghost-write 85% of a book for a friend, who'd promised that if I did so, he and I would engage in a global seminar and workshop tour, bringing these principles to others.

And when I finished the book, the combination of my own depth of understanding of the materials, combined with beautiful marketing design and infrastructure that would allow us to reach tens of thousands of students at once, gave my friend such instant credibility that his ego immediately became engorged. And as such, any time I gently corrected his mistaken and ill-informed view of a particular aspect of the teaching, he became a little more passive-aggressive and started striking back.

In his distorted perspective, he imagined I was trying to control him when I personally didn't care about controlling him in the least. In fact, I never considered it even remotely possible to control him, because he has not yet learned the humility that is required to be led, and as such lacks the humility that is necessary to be a leader as well.

This individual, instead of deepening his understanding of the principles I wrote about in "his" book, decided that scatter his energies and connect with any and every new age quack that came his way, because they could form a mutual admiration society, feed one another's egos, and tell one another how wonderful they were. And in order to justify that kind of genuinely retarded behaviour, he had to publicly decry the information in my own book as being erroneous.

Now that I have demonstrated unequivocally that these principles, which preceded the ancient Hawaiian Huna tradition by almost 800 years, have been a tried and proven training system for eliminating the chaotic data from the subconscious and conscious minds, those who are seriously interested in spiritual growth know who was properly trained, and who was "blowing smoke".

I was disappointed that my friend destroyed any possibility that existed for me to support his desire to teach others. But I remained joy-filled because I was freed from the bad karma that will result from someone inadequately-trained trying to teach information they don't understand and have never personally integrated. And I was also joyful over the realisation that my friend is exactly where he needs and deserves to be so that he can work out his own issues and learn the lessons he needs and wants to learn... even if it's the hard way!

No one puts it quite as succinctly as Geshe Rabten in his book, *Advice from a Spiritual Friend*:

> *If we experience a joyous feeling, even under very adverse situations, this is a sign of attainment in our practice. For example, when we meet another person who unjustly criticizes us, or when we are deeply suffering from an illness or great remorse and, instead of becoming hurt and feeling upset, we spontaneously feel great joy, this is a clear indication that we are becoming well acquainted with the principles of thought transformation.*

> *When we are not in contact with such adverse circumstances, then, of course, we feel happy, calm, and peaceful. Yet if we suffer and become upset just like anyone else when meeting with such difficulties, this clearly shows our practice is deficient and that we should apply still more effort. We do not require an external teacher to determine the effectiveness of our practice since we can each make our own test by assessing our reactions to the specific circumstances we encounter.* (Rabten, 2001)

WITH EXPERIENCE, YOU CAN PRACTICE EVEN WHEN DISTRACTED

"Experienced riders do not fall off their horses," writes His Holiness Dilgo Khyentse Rinpoche, "In the same way, when unexpected harm or sudden difficulties befall us, if love and compassion, rather than annoyance, come welling up in us of their own accord - in other words, if uncomfortable situations can be used to advantage in our lives - that is a sign that we have accomplished something in the Mind Training. So, it is vitally important for us to continue our efforts."

You will know that you are well-trained when you can engage your spiritual practice even in the midst of life's distractions. Atiśa is saying: if you are attentive, that's enough. Be attentive to your inattention, be aware that you have not been aware, that's all. No repentance is needed... Mindfulness and awareness are the keys.

THE EIGHTEEN COMMITMENTS OF MIND TRAINING

Next, we find the Sixth Point: the commitments of mind training:

1. Always abide by the three basic principles:

2. Change your attitude, but remain neutral,

3. Don't be partial, always train in the three general points,

4. Transform your attitude but maintain your natural behaviour,

5. Don't speak of others' incomplete qualities,

6. Don't concern yourself with others' business,

7. Train to counter whichever disturbing emotion is greatest,

8. Give up every hope of reward,

9. Avoid poisonous food,

10. Don't maintain consistency,

11. Don't make sarcastic remarks,

12. Don't lie in ambush,

13. Don't strike at the vital point,

14. Don't burden an ox with the load of a dzo,

15. Don't abuse the practice,

16. Don't sprint to win the race,

17. Don't turn gods into devils,

18. Don't seek others' misery as a means to happiness.

ALWAYS ABIDE BY THE THREE BASIC PRINCIPLES

The three basic principles are also described as [1] keeping your Refuge vows and Bodhisattva vows, [2] refraining from harmful and outrageous action, and [3] developing patience.

The first principle is rather simple and straightforward. We want to remain mindful and renew our Refuge vows and Bodhisattva motivation every day.

The second principle is to guard ourselves against spiritual exhibitionism. We've seen those who get a little taste of what the spiritual life is about, and suddenly, they're prancing about town in their robes, or putting on "dharma classes" at the new age bookstore, when they haven't even begun to fully integrate the teaching themselves.

This is egomaniacal showmanship and a deep violation of integrity and ethics.

And finally, because we will have to encounter people like that... people who are quick to change their Facebook name to their new Dharma name, but who still do nothing to support the teaching, or physically fail to engage their practice by doing anything to alleviate another's suffering... we must cultivate patience. Patience organically gives rise to compassion, and our compassion allows the space in which the other person might grow.

More importantly, patience allows us the space to look more deeply at such situations, and ask ourselves, "What is this situation reflecting from within myself, which I can work on correcting so that this person's experience might be transformed?"

Again... ***100% Responsibility.***

Change Your Attitude, But Remain Neutral

In his book Enlightened Courage, H.H. Dilgo Khyentse Rinpoche explains:

> *From time without beginning, our ego-clinging has caused us to wander in samsara; it is the root of all our sufferings, it is indeed the culprit.*
>
> *Considering others to be more important than ourselves, we should give up our self-cherishing attitudes and decide to act without hypocrisy, emulating in body, speech and mind the*

behaviour of friends who live their lives according to the teachings.

Mind Training should be engaged in discreetly. It should not be done with an external show, in a way that attracts attention and creates a reputation; it should act as the inward antidote to our self-clinging and defiled emotions. We should bring our minds to ripeness without anybody knowing.

REMAIN IMPARTIAL

This point once again is fairly simple: Don't discuss unpleasant subjects. Avoid discussing other people's faults in worldly matters (such as physical or mental disabilities), or their faults in spiritual matters (violations of ordination, for instance). Strive to speak gently and with a spirit of encouragement.

WORK ON YOUR GREATEST OBSTACLES FIRST

If you focus your attention on the bigger challenges -- anger, hostility, violence, or whatever big "defects" that stand in the way of your practice, you will find that many of the smaller obstacles resolve themselves.

This is not about being punitive, but rather about recognising the point of power and creation is always within our minds. Our afflictions are seemingly countless, and since they are active in no other place than within our minds, their destruction can only take place internally as well, because they are not "real" anywhere else!

ABANDON ALL ATTACHMENT TO RESULTS

Engage your spiritual practice as a way of life. The ego-mind is results-oriented. As a result of that, it will always try to find shortcuts, and cunning schemes to avoid doing the work. No one can ghost-write your spiritual memoir for you!

When you return to the moment, there is no preoccupation with future results. It's all about Pure Awareness. As Brian Beresford puts it so well, "When we work to develop the awakening mind, all our efforts must be dedicated for the benefit of all sentient beings. Our practice is impure if we hope for personal gratification and reward. Such hope is not only selfish but is useless and should be renounced. Our personal benefit is a natural side effect from the sincere practice of Dharma performed for the good of all beings."

GIVE UP POISONOUS FOOD

There is a saying: "Wholesome deeds performed with selfish aims are just like poisoned food."

Poisonous foods are a metaphor for the seemingly beautiful and lofty things we take into our minds and practices, which are actually detrimental and toxic to our motivation. For example, if we think, "As long as I can sit in the perfect asana, and perform all the sadhanas perfectly, I will achieve enlightenment and be an exceptional meditator," we are consuming toxic or poisonous foods.

Instead, our attitude must be to resolve to remain in the moment, doing all we can, no matter how frail or small, for the sake of all sentient beings.

B. Allan Wallace, in his brilliant work, *The Seven-Point Mind Training*, writes of this:

> *As we engage in spiritual practice, we pollute our spiritual food with poison by remaining unaware of self-grasping and the egotism and self-centeredness that derive from it. If we do not discard these as enemies that afflict us but instead simply accept them, our practice is like eating poisoned food. There is no question that one can meditate assiduously, translate books and become a great scholar, or even an articulate teacher, and still have self-centeredness at the very core of one's involvement in dharma.*

> *Whether our practice is as profound as Kalacakra, Mahamudra, or Dzogchen, or as straightforward as breath awareness and loving-kindness, if we approach it with a*

mind that is grasping onto the inherent existence of phenomena, it acts as a cause for further cycling in samsara. We may be trying to do something of benefit, but self-grasping pollutes the spiritual practice like a poison. It acts as a cause of further suffering and therefore should be abandoned. (Wallace, 1992)

DON'T RELY ON CONSISTENCY

"A person who is consistent in his affairs doesn't forget the people who concern him, no matter where he is or how much time has gone by. When someone causes you trouble and has made you angry, you might never let go of that resentment. Stop it. Take a helpful attitude or action in response to someone who causes trouble."

- Jamyong Kongtrul Rinpoche

In other words, we should not be so predictable! Allow the Dharma to change your perspective and reshape how you respond to life. If someone hurts you, don't hold onto that poison, and keep drinking it, hoping they will die from it! Just let go. Let them go, and free yourself from the bondage of anger and resentment.

If something nice is done for you, show your gratitude and then let it go. Don't allow yourself to get caught up in the attachment to the ideas of what you did to "deserve" such kindness.

Break free! Be in the moment!

Don't Make Sarcastic Remarks

The first time I heard this maxim, I thought, *"Oh shit! Am I ever in trouble!"* For me, sarcasm isn't just a way to respond, it's an art form!

But it's not casual and well-intended sarcasm that is being challenged here… it's what I call *"reactive sarcasm"*.

Let's look at what His Holiness Dilgo Khyentse Rinpoche has to say about this maxim, for greater clarity:

> *If people say to us, 'You are not a good practitioner. Your vows are useless,' we should not respond, by pointing out their defects, for instance telling a blind man that he is blind, or a lame man that he is a cripple. If we act like this, then both parties will be angry. Therefore, let us not utter a word that will harm or make others unhappy.* (Rinpoche D. K., 1993)

When things are not going well, we should not blame anyone else. Another interpretation of this maxim would be "Do not malign others."

DON'T WAIT IN AMBUSH

This is another powerful one. Imagine if you would that there is a dedicated and serious practitioner who comes to the Dharma centre at a time in her life when she's realised her husband has been unfaithful.

She may readily understand and integrate the teachings of the Dharma in a way that helps her to alleviate the suffering she's experienced, but might keep that little tidbit of info about her husband's transgressions "up her sleeve" in case she "needs to use it one day".

In this case, she's put her entire practice at risk of becoming poison, because she's withholding the most essential of all practices, LETTING GO.

She's grasping that hatred, resentment, and so forth, because she imagines that there is some substantial "self" that was violated. But if she chooses to no longer wait in ambush... to dwell in the present moment... she lets go of all of those past hurts, because they ultimately have no power, sway or influence over her. Her new motivation is to alleviate the suffering of other sentient beings, and that will naturally include her husband.

Don't Strike at the Heart

This is a maxim that goes together with the one we've just discussed. This means letting go of the tendency to rely on spiteful or callous words, in order to inflict an equal measure of pain toward one who hurts us.

I'll tell you that this one has been one of the principle focus-points of my practice because it's the one I struggle most with.

In her book, *Start Where You Are: A Guide to Compassionate Living*, Ani Pema Chodron writes:

These are nuances of the human tragedy, nuances of the tragicomic situation in which we find ourselves. "Don't bring things to a painful point" is again saying, "Don't humiliate people." We do all of these things because we feel pain because we feel hurt and separate. Instead of first making friends with what we're feeling and then, second, trying to communicate, we have all these ways of keeping the "us and them" story solid and strong. That's what causes all the pain on this earth, including the fact that the ecosystem is turned upside down. All of that comes from people not making friends with themselves and never being willing to communicate with the one they consider to be the troublemaker. That's how we stay caught in this battleground, this war zone.

And so we mindfully choose not to strike at the heart... not to look for the weak spot in another's psyche... and not to use our Higher Tantric practice in ways that would bring about harm to ourselves or to others.

DON'T PUT A HORSE'S LOAD ON A PONY

While it may sound rather whimsical, the intention of this maxim is quite serious. When we attempt to shift the burden of something which is our responsibility onto someone else, or when we encounter a problem and attempt to make it someone else's problem, then we are putting a horse's load on a pony. We must take 100% responsibility for those things we encounter in life, and we can only do that by dealing with our own "crap".

Not long ago, I read a post by someone who pretends to be an authority on holistic healing, and *ho'oponopono,* in which he suggested that those who lay false claim to acts of mercy and love will never know the beauty of either until they cease their bad behaviour.

Karmic laws will ensure continued struggle and pain. They will continue to seek all that they purport to share until they learn the lessons.

This was intended as a dig at those who actually wrote the bulk of the works that he now claims to be his own. But what was particularly striking about this "expert's" ignorance was that he pretends to be an authority on *ho'oponopono*, but fails to recognise that the correct response to what he perceives to be "false acts of mercy" ought to have been for him to accept 100% responsibility for the disaster he created, which is manifest in those people's lives.

Sadly, many will be deceived by his charisma and ability to talk in endless circles, without saying anything of any import. But in the end, he will have to come to a reckoning with his responsibility for the karmic seeds he planted.

REMEMBER, THIS IS NOT A COMPETITION

I think that this maxim is best summed up in the words of Chogyam Trungpa Rinpoche, who wrote:

When practitioners begin to develop their understanding of the teaching of the dharma and their appreciation of the dharma, they sometimes fall into a sort of racehorse approach. Such practitioners are concerned with who can do their prostrations faster, who can sit better, who can eat better, who can do this and that better.

But if our practice is regarded purely as a race, we have a problem. The whole thing has become a game rather than an actual practice, and there is no seed of benevolence and gentleness in the practitioner. So, you should not use your practice as a way to get ahead of your fellow students.

In a horse race, the aim is to be the fastest. The study of Dharma is not a horserace. The purpose of the training is not to set down laws and regulations, but simply to derive benefit. Have no concern about receiving or not receiving recognition or prestige. (Rinpoche C. T., 1981)

You may never be the esteemed guest of honour at a metaphysical bookstore and might not have as many "fans" on Facebook, but you will have achieved what those persons could not... peace and calm abiding.

Do Not Misuse the Remedy

If we were to engage in a practice so that others might call us "Bodhisattvas", or in order to appear to be a great martyr, thus trying to build up our reputation, then we are abusing the privilege of practising the Dharma.

Even to engage in practice for the purpose of curing ourselves of some sort of affliction would be considered the misuse of the remedy. Mind Training is not some sort of sorcery or magical formula for happiness. It is a path that frees us from the afflictions that cause us to suffer so that we, in turn, might alleviate the suffering of all sentient beings.

As Alan Wallace observes, "Being devious, cunning, or sly has no place in a life that is oriented towards dharma."

Do Not Turn the Sacred into the Profane

The idea of this maxim is that we should not make painful what is already inherently joyful. It is a prescription against dwelling on our pain and misfortune and going through life as a great martyr.

It also means that we should not ever allow our spiritual attainments to become something we "show-off" because that would be turning something beautiful into something ugly.

DON'T SEEK ANOTHER'S SUFFERING AS A MEANS OF PERSONAL GAIN

We've all witnessed the disgrace that occurs when someone dies, and their surviving family members scramble and fight over who will get what, of their belongings, their money, their property, etc.

This maxim extends to such circumstances as well as the equally disgraceful tendency to perform Dharma rituals or ceremonies with the intention of personal gain. For example, if one's student has a dying parent, and a practitioner was to eagerly await that person's passing so that they could be paid to do the funeral, that is taking advantage of another's suffering.

Likewise, if we encourage the wrong behaviour of a student or friend, simply so that we can seem to be "important" or "wise counsel", then we are taking advantage of another's suffering.

Again, Alan Wallace offers wise insight:

> *This final precept may be pertinent for many of us. The commentator provides several examples, one of which concerns inheritance. Anticipating the death of a relative or rich friend in hopes of benefiting is certainly a case of seeking another's misery for the sake of your own happiness.*

Another major example concerns people whom we cannot stand. We may be gladdened at the prospect of an enemy dying, or falling into disgrace, or getting hit by a truck. Our imagination can become very fertile here, but such thoughts are to be abandoned.

Sechibuwa also gives as an example a meditator or dharma teacher vying for reputation with others in the same region, thinking that the illness or death of a peer would result in greater respect or more offerings for oneself. This brings to mind contemporary examples from business or academia, where people compete for their own happiness to the detriment of their colleagues. The arena of sex provides other examples: breaking up a harmonious relationship because of lust for one of the people involved. The envy and selfishness of such actions are tragic.

Whether an enemy meets with misfortune, sickness, or death, is a matter of his or her own karma. Our own history and past actions determine the fortune or misfortune presented to each of us. Wishing misfortune on someone does not cause that misfortune to happen. Instead, because the yearning for another person's suffering is itself an unwholesome mental action, it immediately places unwholesome imprints upon our own mind and guarantees

our own future suffering if those imprints are not purified.
(Wallace, 1992)

TWENTY ONE GUIDELINES

The final section of mind training offers general guidelines, which include what to reject and what to adopt as we make our Dharmic journey.

ALL PRACTICES SHOULD BE DONE WITH ONE INTENTION.

This one intention is to awaken bodhicitta, to awaken the heart. Practice here includes the training of meditation in the post-meditation state: In whatever you do - sitting, walking, eating, drinking, even sleeping - you should always take the attitude of being of benefit to all sentient beings. In other words, whatever activities we do, there is one way to focus, one way to practice. In this particular context of mind training, it means being benevolent, and this implies never parting from the good-will of wanting to benefit others in all that we do.

CORRECT ALL WRONGS WITH ONE INTENTION

Whenever something difficult or some painful circumstance happens, be it sickness, frustration, having others malign our reputation or resistance to our practice, we should cultivate compassion for all sentient beings who suffer these same circumstances, aspiring to take on their suffering through the practice of *tonglen*.

The next instruction tells us how to deal with these misfortunes:

TWO THINGS TO BE DONE - AT THE START AND END

The third point has to do with how we conduct ourselves on a daily basis.

I find it necessary to remind myself often, and rely on the words of His Holiness Dilgo Khyentse Rinpoche, who advises on this maxim:

> *In the morning, on waking, we should make the following pledge: 'Throughout the whole of today, I will remember Bodhicitta. Eating, dressing, meditating, wherever I go, I will practice it constantly. Should it slip my mind, I will remind myself. Mindful of it, I will not allow myself to wander into states of anger, desire or ignorance.'*

> *We should make a concerted effort to keep this vow and at night, before going to sleep, we should examine ourselves as to how much we have been able to generate Bodhicitta, how much we have been able to help others and whether all our actions have been in accordance with the teachings, confessing the day's faults and resolving that, from the next day onwards, within 24 hours, or a month, or at least within a year, we will have some signs of improvement.*

We should steel ourselves so as not to be daunted by the work of abandoning defects. If during the day our actions have not been contrary to the teachings and we have maintained an altruistic attitude, then we should be happy, thinking, 'Today has been a useful day, I have remembered what my teacher has taught me and this is to accomplish his wishes. Tomorrow I will do better than today, and even better the day after.' This is how to ensure the growth of our Bodhicitta.

REGARDLESS OF THE OUTCOME, BE PATIENT

To simplify, we can say that there are only two outcomes to any situation: positive or negative. If bad things happen, we should not blame anyone else: it is our own misfortune coming from our own karma.

This is why we practice *ho'oponopono or* taking 100% responsibility for everything that occurs in our lives.

If good things happen, then we should not gloat or relax our practice, but rather take the opportunity to mindfully wish that these good things happen to others as well.

This also means that whatever good happens to us, such as wealth, power, or influence, we must always use these experiences for the good of all sentient beings.

Khenchen Thrangu Rinpoche teaches, "Because of being too fond of having a good time and enjoying ourselves, it is quite likely that we should forget about our concern for other beings and become insensitive. If things always go wrong and we continuously have problems, it is quite likely that we will get caught up in that and worry about ourselves too much. The instructions here are to be willing to be patient with whatever happens, whether good or bad times."

Whatever happens, we should:

MAINTAIN THESE TWO, EVEN AT THE RISK OF YOUR LIFE

This maxim refers once again to the refuge and bodhisattva vows. It has a sense of urgency -"even at the risk of your life" - Pema Chodron tells us that is means not to be afraid to leave the nest or be afraid of losing ground or of things falling apart or of not having it all together.

We recognise that all present and future happiness is the direct result of faithfully observing the Dharma principles transmitted to us by our qualified teacher or teachers, as well as adhering to the commitments of mind training. All of these are contained within the five precepts and the fourteen precepts of mindfulness.

We should always maintain all of our *Samaya* commitments.

Samayas or commitments are essential in that they aid the practitioner in refraining from mistakes which, if engaged in, would damage his or her practice and thus counteract progress on the path.

When a student is initiated (called the *abhiśeka* ceremony) they create (through vows) a bond between the guru and themselves.

There are fourteen root downfalls, which constitute the breaking of Samaya — a karmically dangerous and serious offense, which jeopardises and can legitimise one's entire Dharma practice.

These vows pertain specifically to the *anuttarayoga tantra* class of practices; they are incurred after one has received an *abhiṣeka* into that class of practices.

The fourteen vows described by Sakya Pandita, as elucidated by Shamar Rinpoche,[5] are transgressed by the following fourteen root downfalls:

1. **Physically harming or slandering the teacher from whom one received the abhiśeka** – The following conditions must be present for the Samaya to be broken: one must be fully aware of one's actions and intend them, be aware that they will displease the teacher, and fail to regret them. With intention but no follow-through, only a breach is committed. Further, the severity of the breach is considered small, average or great depending on whether or not the student has received abhiṣeka, explanations

and pith instructions—if just the former it is small, if the first two it is average, and if all three it is great.

2. **Opposing the words of the buddhas** – Denigrating enlightened wisdom teachings.

3. **Strong negative emotions towards one's vajra brothers and sisters** – Becoming strongly hostile towards men and women who have received *abhiśeka* from the same teachers as oneself.

4. **Abandoning loving kindness and compassion for sentient beings**.

5. **Abandoning the *bodhichitta*** in aspiration or application.

6. **Criticising other traditions.**

7. **Revealing secrets to those who are unworthy.** "If one describes the meaning of great bliss as taught in Vajrayana to individuals who do not possess the required educational background, they might misunderstand and abuse these teachings."

8. **Mistreating one's body**. "The human body is the support for dharma practice, the basis upon which realization of the two buddhakayas is attained. With respect to Vajrayana, the human body is considered to be an important instrument on the path. Therefore, exposing the body to extreme conditions such as

whipping, burning or destroying it by suicide, contributes to the breaking of the Samaya." The human body is the support for dharma practice, the basis upon which realisation of the two *buddhakayas* is attained. With respect to Vajrayana, the human body is considered to be an important instrument on the path.

For example, if a student is hospitalised for a medical condition, and learns that disgusting personal habits, such as smoking, overeating, or not properly caring for one's body, will make the condition worse; if they do not correct those habituations, they are guilty of this downfall.

9. **Abandoning emptiness.**

10. **Keeping bad company**. Associating with Samaya corrupters.

11. **Failing to reflect on emptiness.**

12. **Upsetting those who have faith in the teachings**.

13. **Failing to observe the Samaya commitments**.

14. **Denigrating women**. Shamar Rinpoche writes, "Within Vajrayana women are considered to be the embodiment of wisdom. Regarding women as inferior or abusing them as witnessed in certain cultures, contributes to the breaking of the Samaya."

Jamgon Kongtrul Rinpoche comments on the *Lamrim Yeshe Ningpo* that Samaya is established by taking *abhiṣeka* and *Samaya* is the manner in which practitioners "preserve the life-force of that empowerment within your being". Breaking these commitments removes all the benefits of one's Dharma practice. As Khenpo Karthar Rinpoche teaches, "the most egregious root samaya to violate is the commitment to one's guru."

According to Tulku Urgyen Rinpoche, there are four increasing stages in which one's samaya may be damaged: "infraction, breach, violation, and complete break". Once damaged, samaya may be repaired. But if it is left without repair for more than three years, it is irreparable.

Samaya is easily damaged. Patrul Rinpoche said it is very hard to maintain samaya, and used a famous metaphor that maintaining Samaya is like keeping a mirror or tile clean that is lifted up into a sand storm; dust settles on it as soon as it is clean and we must continuously clean it.

To repair samaya, a practitioner may restore mindfulness and awareness of sacred view; confess the violation to another practitioner that holds samaya; recite the one hundred syllable mantra (Vajrasattva mantra), or use other methods determined by their guru. They must then take the steps to restore those commitments and return to the lotus feet of their guru. If they refuse, then they will suffer the karmic consequences of their actions.

For those whose spiritual maturity is severely lacking, and who after breaking samaya with their guru, claim to be returning to a "solitary practice", unguided by a qualified teacher, the danger of breaking samaya is exponentially increased, because such practitioners, without a qualified teacher, are enrapt in nothing more than the egocentric appearance of being "devout and holy practitioners," while in reality, their own arrogance, immaturity, and excuses have been used to justify disgracing their commitments, turning their back on their teacher, who is the embodiment of the Buddha, the Dharma and the Sangha.

Therefore, no matter what they would like to pretend, they have turned their back on the Buddha, the Dharma and the Sangha, the moment they broke samaya.

It should be noted that simply disagreeing with one's teacher is not breaking samaya. Even if one's actions are in discord with a teacher's instructions, for example, if a morbidly obese student wishes to pretend that they are just "overweight", this does not jeopardise their practice, it simply means they are in denial and refuse to accept simple medical facts. No samaya is broke since this is just a sign of psychological weakness and ignorance.

Samaya is broken when the following conditions are present:

- one is fully aware of a lama to be his or her guru and consciously physically or verbally harms this person,

- awareness that one's actions will displease the guru,

- feeling no regret after having harmed the guru.

His Eminence Tsem Tulku Rinpoche offers key insights on why this breaking of samaya is dangerous:

Teacher samaya is very special to me. Good relations and good samaya with one's guru can never be overstressed in our growth for spiritual practices. If we don't keep good relations with our guru, then our mind will degenerate. How does it degenerate? We find samsaric activities more and more 'pleasurable'. We find our daily routine activities 'safe'. We are able to find more and more excuses for ourselves to justify and do our best to convince others that we are fine, we will do Dharma later or that we are doing the 'best' we can now. In fact, people can see through our excuses. But they are too polite to say more...

But in actuality we are drifting further and farther away from our practice, Dharma thoughts, Dharma activities and especially Dharma growth within our mindstream. Sometimes we are able to see the degeneration happen, but due to broken unrepaired samaya, we do nothing about it even though we see it. Conviction in Dharma that was very strong before becomes intellectual knowledge used to 'debate' with others to protect our degenerated position.

When our samaya further degenerates then we start developing the wrong view of our teacher even though our teacher may have been very helpful and beneficial in our lives in the past.

When our samaya further degenerates then we start developing the wrong view of our teacher even though our teacher may have been very helpful and beneficial in our lives in the past. In some cases, the teacher has saved our livelihood, lives and even sanity. We start to have mental and physical distance. Why? Outwardly it is to show that 'I am not happy' with our teacher, but inwardly we know that we have degenerated, and we are angry and ashamed to face our teacher and other students. It is hard to face the cold hard facts that we know to be true. Blaming other students for our distance is another cover for laziness, jealousy and anger.

Why? What Bodhisattva-aspirant hates their perceived enemies? Or blames their enemies?

Seeing our teacher point-blank reminds us of our degeneration. The other students working hard, doing well in their Dharma pursuits and activities remind us of what we're supposed to do but are not doing. Therefore, we avoid or go deeper into our so-called beneficial activities in our mundane lives.

In extreme cases, even boiling jealousy may arise when we hear other students are successful in their Dharma work and pursuits. Why would jealousy arise? Because we have used Dharma to feed our ego and to look good. Looking good is to fill an empty void that we feel inside. That empty void exists because there is a gnawing feeling that we have not done something really worthwhile with our lives. This would eat at us. Sometimes in our degenerated state, we wish to teach our teacher a 'lesson' or 'punish' our teacher for not giving us WHAT WE WANTED; so, we stay away or do not cooperate. But the whole point of a teacher is not to give us what we want but what we ACTUALLY NEED. After all, that is why we call it a teacher-disciple relationship.

When we degenerate in our relationship with our teacher, degeneration in our Dharma practice WILL DEFINITELY FOLLOW. It is, unfortunately, a natural process. Then we are left with just the mundane activities of daily life that we try to seek 'refuge' and comfort in. Engaging in familiar mundane activities may temporarily 'soothe' our mind for the time being, but it deceptively takes a toll on our time that is fast running out. No one lives forever. Not the teacher nor the students. We end up hiding behind our daily mundane activities and cover-up by telling people that WE ARE VERY BUSY. But in fact, we are no busier than other Dharma students who are doing the same mundane activities we are doing daily COMBINED WITH THEIR DHARMA WORK / PRACTICE simultaneously.

The final instruction concerns disturbing emotions:

TRAIN IN THE THREE AUSTERITIES

To eliminate disturbing emotions there are three things we can do: first, we must recognise our neurosis as neurosis; then we must apply the mind training, and a correct dharmic antidote to overcome the neurosis. Every neurosis stems from self-cherishing, and so we must, therefore, release our tendency to be selfish. The final "austerity" is to resolve not to allow ourselves to fall victim to that neurosis again.

There are three preliminary conditions or causes for a successful Dharma practice:

Take Up the Three Primary Conditions

Khenchen Thrangu Rinpoche teaches on these three primary conditions beautifully:

These three causes are: (a) relying on an authentic teacher; (b) settling our mind very firmly in the dharma so that it becomes workable; and (c) having the necessary materials to practice, such as clothes, food, implements, and time. We must work to have all these circumstances come together for us. This has to do with not turning away from the seeds mentioned.

The first cause is a genuine spiritual teacher who is realized. We should not have trust in someone who acts contrary to the spiritual teachings. Let's say we have met someone who teaches something that is correct, invaluable, and worthy. This essential trust ensures that we can practice. If we don't trust the teachings and the teacher, then how can we carry through with the instructions? So that sense of trust is something to keep, and we should not let it slip away.

The second cause is to have enthusiasm for mind training, delight in practising and applying the instructions, having understood their value, and, finally, being happy to continue. The third cause is not to turn away from mind training itself, not to forget what is to be avoided and what is to be adopted.

When this is done:

Pay Attention That These Three Things Do Not Diminish

There are three things that we should never allow to diminish in our practice. First, because the guru is the root of all virtue, we should not let our trust for him or her ever diminish.

Second, because mind training teachings are essential to the Mahayana tradition, we should not let our joy and delight in practising these teachings ever diminish.

Finally, because our desire is to eliminate suffering and the causes of suffering for all sentient beings, we should not let any of our vows diminish.

KEEP THE THREE INSEPARABLE QUALITIES

We should also make sure that virtuous activity is inseparable from body, speech, and mind. This is quite simple and straightforward.

Next, we should:

TRAIN IMPARTIALLY IN ALL AREAS

I could not put it more succinctly than the advice of Khenchen Thrangu Rinpoche, who teaches:

Being impartial is how we train in loving-kindness and compassion: we don't favour those who deserve our love and compassion or turn our backs on others. Rather, we make no distinctions in being kind and compassionate.

It is said we should be impartial in all areas of our practice and not limit ourselves. The second aspect is to make this pervasive: there is no barrier or limitation to any area of our training in how we regard others. We train totally to embrace everyone. It also means that we do not look outside, but rather at our own hearts and minds. Whenever it is difficult to be loving and kind, we work to overcome that barrier. When we feel like holding back our compassion, we train to overcome this withdrawal.

We should not just practice mind training and compassion towards one living being while overlooking another. Mind training and bodhichitta should apply to all human and non-human beings without exception.

ALWAYS MEDITATE ON WHAT YOU RESENT

This one was a biggie for me! When we have an opponent or someone we don't like, it is harder to feel love and compassion. Instead of allowing the resentments that arise in our minds to become an obstacle, we use them as fuel for our practice. We assume 100% responsibility for our experiences and recall that whatever aggravates us is merely a reflection of something on the subconscious level that we have yet to resolve.

Chogyam Trungpa Rinpoche offers sage advice in this regard:

> *If we really want to communicate, we have to give up knowing what to do. When we come in with our agendas, they only block us from seeing the person in front of us. It's best to drop our five-year plans and accept the awkward sinking feeling that we are entering a situation naked. We don't know what will happen next or what we'll do.*

The remaining guidelines, while simple and requiring little further commentary are equally important.

DON'T BE SWAYED BY OUTER CIRCUMSTANCES.

Always remain mindful that whatever appears in our experience is but a reflection of the chaotic data playing on the subconscious level. It is merely an opportunity for us to clear away one more delusion.

PRACTICE WHAT IS MOST IMPORTANT.

We have attained a precious human birth and come into contact with the dharma, so we have the most important elements necessary to practice.

AVOID MAKING MISTAKES.

In our practice, we are trying to develop the qualities of trust, devotion, kindness, and compassion. We should be diligent to avoid situations or circumstances that will conflict with this stated objective.

THE FINAL REMINDERS

In addition, we are told:

- Don't Waiver.

- Train with your Whole Heart.

- Free Yourself through Examination and Self-analysis.

- Don't Make a Big Deal About Your Practice or Your Self

- Don't Let Being Irritated Throw You Off-Course

- Stay Focused.

- Don't Expect a Standing Ovation.

All twenty-one points are about the same principle—having a good heart, a good intention, or a noble resolve. And doing these things without expectation of reward, recognition or applause.

The essence of the nectar-like instructions for transforming into the path of awakening the five prevalent signs of degeneration was passed down from the one from Golden Isle. When karmic seeds left over from former trainings were aroused in me, I felt great interest, and so, without regard for suffering or disparagement, I sought instructions on subduing ego-clinging. Now, even in death, I shall have no regrets.

Chapter Two - The Seven Hermetic Principles of the Kybalion

Chief among the pursuits of the practitioner of magick and the occult is often found the desire to look into our philosophical past and spiritual past for clues that might act as a springboard for our diving deeply into the waters of personal and spiritual mastery.

Such pursuits often lead us to rediscover a once-great tradition, which lead to an overall greater understanding of the universe, our place in it, and which became the catalyst for such things the Italian Renaissance, the American Revolution, the New Thought and Enlightenment Movements, and which now shows up in much of modern-day personal growth media.

I'm talking, of course, about Hermeticism.

What Is Hermeticism?

The hermetic tradition represents a pre-Christian lineage of Gnosticism, which is the name for a variety of ancient religious ideas and systems dating back to the first and second centuries in the Common Era.

The term *'Hermetica'* is used to cover a heterogeneous body of works attributed to the legendary philosopher Hermes Trismegistus. The Hermetic works are mostly philosophical, theosophical, astrological, magical or alchemical in nature.

The treatises we now call the *Corpus Hermeticum*, which is today perhaps the best-known Hermetic work, were compiled mainly in the 2nd-3rd centuries CE and have been preserved in Greek codices (although Coptic fragments have also been recovered in Nag Hammadi in 1945).

In the Middle Ages, only one Hermetic work, the Latin Asclepius (its Greek original is lost) was widely known. This changed when Marsilio Ficino in 1463 translated fourteen Greek Hermetic texts into Latin at the request of his patron Cosimo de Medici. The title he gave to this work attributed to Hermes Trismegistus was: *Pimander, sive De potestate et sapientia Dei.*

'Pimander' was the protagonist of the first treatise, after whom Ficino subsequently named the entire work: he believed the *Corpus Hermeticum* to be a single Hermetic text instead of a body of separate treatises.

The **incomplete** codex from which Ficino translated had been brought to Florence from Macedonia by an Italian monk, Leonardo di Pistoia.

This Hermetic text aroused great interest, as Hermes Trismegistus at the time was perceived to be a pagan contemporary of the law-giver Moses.

Thus, the wisdom and revelations Hermes Trismegistus transmitted were regarded as pre-Christian and yet seemed to announce Christianity: as a result, Hermes Trismegistus was celebrated as a pagan prophesying the coming of Christ.

HERMETIC TREATISES

The Hermetic texts in the *Corpus Hermeticum* and the *Asclepius* are not uniform in tone: they contain demonstrably Greek, gnostic and Jewish elements (e.g. discussions on the soul, or the parallel with Genesis in *Corpus Hermeticum I*, the nous in *Corpus Hermeticum IV* corresponding with the gnostic pneuma).

In addition, the treatises are also inspired by Egyptian traditions, as witnessed by the element of the transmission of teachings by a 'father' to his 'son'; as in Egyptian hymns, there is mention of a God who is 'All and One'.

It is a postulate found in most of the Hermetic texts that because of his (*divine*) intellect, man is capable to behold the Cosmos in his mind, to comprehend the divine essence of nature and to imprint it on his soul. By beholding the cosmos it is possible to know *The Unknowable One*: the universe is thus often presented as a text or a book which must be read or deciphered. A very representative Hermetic saying is: *'God is an immortal man, man is a mortal god'*.

PRISCA THEOLOGIA

The idea of a *'prisca theologia'* originates in the Renaissance: a tradition of spiritual wisdom running from Hermes Trismegistus via Moses to Zoroaster, Orpheus, Pythagoras and Plato.

The works of these ancient sages were regarded as divinely inspired and paving the way for Christ. Although Hermes Trismegistus was the first amongst these 'prisci theologi', Ficino also included Zoroaster, Orpheus, Pythagoras and the Pythagorean Philolaus of Croton.

HERMETICA IN THE EARLY MIDDLE AGES

The main authors with links to the Hermetica collected in this period are Boethius (480-ca. 525) and the neo-Platonist Dionysius (second half of the 5th century). The works of Dionysius (erroneously attributed to the Dionysius Areopagita occurring in Acts 17: 34) only became fully accessible to the West in the edition of Johannes Scotus Eriugena, who translated the entire Corpus Dionysiacum around 860.

Renaissance of the Hermetica in the 12th century

The influence of texts attributed to Hermes Trismegistus in the 12th century has been established in the works of theologians and philosophers such as Peter Abelard, Alain de Lille, William of Auvergne, Albertus Magnus and Thomas of York.

The main Hermetic source text to be studied in this seminal period before the Italian Renaissance was the *Asclepius* (which was preserved in Latin), in addition to (pseudo-) Hermetic texts such as the *Liber XXIV philosophorum*, a collection of definitions and commentaries on the nature of God, and the *cosmological Liber de VI rerum principiis.*

We also find in this period the first translations (mainly from the Arabic) of astrological and magical works, such as the Picatrix and the work of Al-Kindi (800-866). Al-Kindi wrote in one of his works that he saw a work by Hermes Trismegistus on the unity of God which no philosopher can deny.

The 'Italian Renaissance' of the Hermetica

In addition to the *Corpus Hermeticum*, the works of the *'prisci theologi'* were enthusiastically studied in the Italian Renaissance.

An important person in this context is Georgius Gemistus, who called himself Pletho to express his reverence for Plato. Pletho's deep admiration for Plato, the Platonists and Zoroaster caused Cosimo de' Medici to found a Platonic Academy in Florence.

The idea of a 'prisca theologia' as expressed by Ficino in the dedication to his translation of the *Corpus Hermeticum* probably derives from Pletho. Ficino's main translating interests concerned Plato and the Neoplatonists (a.o. Plotinus). His own works were also greatly inspired by Neoplatonic thought.

HERMETICA 16TH-18TH CENTURIES

Hermetic thought is one of the factors contributing to the reform movement of (natural) philosophy and science spreading from Italy throughout Europe.

The physician Paracelsus, a follower of Hermes Trismegistus (he was known as 'Trismegistus Germanus') was a key figure in this context. Paracelsus strongly believed in the power of the 'arcana' in the healing process. According to him, these hidden macrocosmic powers could work their effect on man, the microcosm, having the power to change, renovate and restore not only the body but also the patient's mind.

The Englishman Robert Fludd, in whose work the divine light was a central theme, was a Paracelsist and a follower of Hermes Trismegistus – he often refers to Hermetic works, for instance in his Mosaicall philosophy.

In the 17th century Amsterdam was a haven for enlightened thinkers; the works of Spinoza a.o. are printed here. This subsection also includes the works of advocates of religious tolerance (e.g. Castellio, Comenius, Coornhert).

HERMETICA 19TH CENTURY-PRESENT

An impressive culmination of the Hermetic tradition at the end of the 18th century is to be found in the Geheime Figuren der Rosenkreuzer.

In the 19th and 20th centuries, too, the Hermetic texts remained one of the factors shaping Western thought. In the 19th century, new Hermetic societies were formed claiming a Graeco-Egyptian (Hellenistic) origin.

The Hermetic Order of the Golden Dawn (1887), for instance, drew its inspiration from Christian-Hermetic thought as well as Freemasonry and magic. The English scholar A.E. Waite has his own sub-section within the Hermetica because he contributed to every conceivable esoteric field during his long and successful career. New editions of classical Hermetic texts, as well as fresh philosophical, esoteric and literary interpretations and studies, appear to the present day.

The study of the Hermetica received a new impetus in the 20th century, while 19th-century editions of source texts are still frequently reprinted. Especially the publications of A.E. Waite and G.R.S. Mead have encouraged new scholarly studies to appear in the broader field of the Hermetica.

In the 2nd half of the 20th century, a number of important Hermetic texts were discovered in European libraries, including the so-called Hermetica of Oxford and the Definitions of Hermes Trismegistus.

"Master of all arts and sciences, perfect in all crafts, Ruler of the Three Worlds, Scribe of the Gods, and Keeper of the Books of Life, Thoth Hermes Trismegistus—the Three Times Greatest, the "First Intelligencer"—was regarded by the ancient Egyptians as the embodiment of the Universal Mind. While in all probability there actually existed a great sage and educator by the name of Hermes, it is impossible to extricate the historical man from the mass of legendary accounts which attempt to identify him with the Cosmic Principle of Thought." -Manly P. Hall—The Secret Teachings of All Ages (Hall, 1988)

THE FIRST PRINCIPLE – THE PRINCIPLE OF MENTALISM

Within the Kybalion, we first read that all Substantial Reality – that is to say, the outward manifestations, phenomena, and appearances we refer to as "the material universe", is comprised of the same "Spirit".

This "Spirit" is described as "unknowable" and "undefinable". It was neither created, nor can it be destroyed. And it is referred to in the ancient text as the "Universal, Infinite, Living Mind".

In the postmodern world, what is it that we refer to when we talk about something that can neither be created nor destroyed, but which simple changes form?

The idea that "empty" space can have intrinsic energy associated to it, and that there is no such thing as a "true vacuum", ultimately led to the discovery of "dark energy", which Einstein referred to as "zero-point energy".

Zero-point energy can best be understood as that vast, unquantifiable, and indestructible reservoir of "dark matter" from which all manifest phenomena are created. It is the mother of all atomic structure and is the birther of the cosmos.

In the Kybalion, we read that "the Universe is simply a Mental Creation" which exists in the Universal Mind.

In other words, it is a **Thought**.

The New Thought movement is a movement which developed in the United States in the 19th century, considered by many to have been derived from the unpublished writings of Phineas Quimby. Quimby learned about the power of the mind to heal through hypnosis when he observed Charles Poyen's work.

Another influential thinker and teacher at that time were Neville Goddard. Neville Goddard was Teacher of New Thought, who challenged the belief that the bible was based upon historical fact and taught that manifesting desires was possible through the principle of thought or affirmative "prayer". He was brilliant, but for my tastes, a bit too "religious" in the framing of New Thought.

Dr Ernest Holmes, the author of *The Science of Mind*, formulated a five-step process for intentional creation, known as Spiritual Mind Treatment. During the process of a Spiritual Mind Treatment, also known as Affirmative Prayer, Scientific Prayer or simply 'Treatment', we come to the realisation that within the universe there is one Infinite, Universal Presence that permeates everything, and therefore this Presence, being everywhere, has to be right within us, as well.

With this "singular focus" of mind, we reach an acceptance of new possibilities in life, we are able to 'see', 'feel' and speak of the good we desire as already ours.

A 'Treatment' is not about convincing a God(dess) to do something for us. It is becoming aware of our True Nature... the Sacred Presence within ourselves.

The interesting thing about Dr Holmes' process is that it nearly identically can be found to mirror the manner in which any occult practitioner, but particularly Witches, go about Conscious Creation in their spellcasting.

THE SPIRITUAL MIND TREATMENT PROCESS

Step one: We acknowledge that within the universe there is ONE pervading presence, ONE force encompassing everything that is in existence, ONE energy from which all things are made of. Many people throughout the ages have called this Source of all things, God(dess), Spirit, Thought or Universal Mind. The name is not important, what matters is that we recognise this truth.

Step two: Having recognised the magnificence and awesome power of the ONE presence that is absolutely everywhere within the universe, we realise that this same intelligence that created everything, does not stop being where we are. Therefore, It is within us; It is the substance that life is made of. In this step, we become aware of who we really are: A Divine Being made of God(dess)'s energy and having a human experience.

Step three: We name our desire(s) with the feeling that as we do this, it is already ours. We are moving away from the feeling of 'wanting' to the feeling of 'having' already received.

Step four: We summon, from within ourselves, a feeling of gratitude. Of course, the Source of 'ALL That Is', does not need our gratitude to function; it is rather that an attitude of gratitude opens our consciousness to receiving even more good. As the Law of the universe is such that what we focus on, is what we manifest in our experience, when we are focused on the good that we already have, then we can only attract more good.

Step five: Once we have accomplished the four previous steps, all we need to do is trust. We release it to the wisdom and the love of the universe. The Universal Mind does not require our input on 'how' our desire is manifesting itself for us!

THE ANCIENT & UNNAMED PATH

If we examine this idea more closely, it should resonate with us, as practitioners of witchcraft, magick, alchemy and other esoteric paths.

The process of conscious creation or manifestation of phenomena was known to be among the most fundamental aspects of mastery within the Craft of the Wise, as spells and incantations.

An incantation is a magical formula intended to trigger a magical effect on a person, situation, or objects. The formula can be spoken, sung or chanted. An incantation can also be performed during ceremonial rituals or prayers. These spells or charms could also be simply called what they are: esoteric commands to control the phenomenal (and numenal) world.

WHAT PRECEDES OUR SPEECH?

Before you or I can speak a word, we must first think – set our intention, and give energy – to the words we are about to speak.

This is something that witches and practitioners of other magickal arts do mindfully.

So whether you were initiated into a particular tradition, learned the Craft from your hereditary elders, picked up a book, or intuitively began to practice, you were harnessing the power of words, born from intentionality or thought, every time you cast a spell, worked a ritual or offered a prayer.

What if the ancient texts from a multitude of traditions, going back as many as 5,000 years, got it right?

What if the phenomenal and noumenal universes were entirely made up of a single, unquantifiable, dark matter, as Einstein observed... and that matter was what the New Thought teachers called "Thought" or "Universal Mind"?

What if the "secret" to a fruitful and rich practice of the Craft was not the non-sensical, ego-driven, fanboy/fangirl bullshit about lineage, heredity, and all of the other bullshit we derive from television and fictional stories, myths and legends we were told?

And instead, that "secret" was to shut the fuck up, and go to work on mastering our mind... learning the intrinsic synergy between the cycle of the seasons and our experiences in life... cultivating the wisdom of calm abiding, and knowing that our thoughts create our experiences?

SIFTING THROUGH THE CHAOTIC DATA

- Out of chaos comes regeneration.

- The birth of new ideas and mastery of our innate power has never depended on heredity, hierarchy, religious superstition, period costume, "lineage" or origin of tradition.

- Your birthright is the same as every other being on the planet, both "animate" and "inanimate".

- Until you master the First Principle of Hermetics, you are not practising magick.

THE SECOND PRINCIPLE – THE HERMETIC PRINCIPLE OF CORRESPONDENCE

The actual text of that maxim, as translated by Dennis W. Hauck from *The Emerald Tablet of Hermes Trismegistus*, is:

"That which is Below corresponds to that which is Above, and that which is Above corresponds to that which is Below, to accomplish the miracle of the One Thing." (Hauk, 2013)

The Principle of Correspondence basically says that our current reality is a mirror of what is going on inside us. Our reality is a result of our innermost dominant thoughts and beliefs.

It does not mean that if our lives are filled with unhappiness, chaos or are just straight up unfulfilling, it is because that's how we are on the inside... or that it's our fault.

That is not metaphysics... it's ignorant new age fluff. There have been books written that say otherwise, and entire movements that shame those who are poor, sick, and even abused, and it's repugnant.

As Within, So Without

This principle really says that our current reality is a mirror of what is going on inside us.

If, for example, we suffer from low self-esteem, our experience of the world will be interpreted through the lens of that belief system.

If we believe that the world is a cold and hostile place, we tend to interpret our experiences through the lens of that belief as well. But what happens when we choose to think differently?

The Fundamental Premise

We are all governed by a set of universal laws and principles, and when we are not operating in alignment with these laws, nature will have a way of letting us know, so that we can adjust our mindsets, beliefs and actions.

Our experiences are not changed by placing blame. Blame will not change the past, and it never creates a solution for the present moment. In essence, when we place blame, we are actually trying to escape dealing with the root cause of our suffering. Chaotic data can cloud the lens through which we interpret these experiences.

CORRESPONDENCE BETWEEN WHAT, EXACTLY?

The principle tells us that there is a direct correspondence between spiritual laws and the manifestation of phenomena.

There are planes beyond our knowledge, but when we understand Universal Principles, it places us back in our own power.

This is about assuming 100% responsibility for our lives. The Principle of Correspondence enables us to reason intelligently from the microcosm to the macrocosm and back again.

It does not matter what we change on the outside, if we haven't done the work to change on the inside, our reality will continue to reflect what's going on inside us.

Only when we shift within can our experiences evolve to become a reflection of our new inner beliefs and worldview. While this universal principle works on all planes, for all persons equally, it does not mean it's someone's "fault" if something goes wrong.

While this universal principle works on all planes, for all persons equally, it does not mean it's someone's "fault" if something goes wrong.

The person born in poverty in Appalachia did nothing wrong to create those circumstances.

The person who is sexually assaulted did not get raped because they thought poor thoughts.

Someone who dies from cancer didn't lack the right belief, power or "skill" to cure themselves.

It also is not a principle designed to be used as justification for New Age ableism, or the ego-driven desire to appear more spiritually evolved because someone lacks the commitment to stand up for social justice principles.

Political neutrality might sell more books, tapes and workshops, but it's definitely not a sign of an evolved mind or spiritual maturity. In fact, it is quite the opposite.

TAKE-AWAYS

Magick is nothing if not learning to work with your beliefs, thoughts, and energies to live in greater harmony with nature and the cosmos.

As witches and sorcerers, we don't change things... we work with the energy around things, circumstances, beliefs, etc. to create an atmosphere in which our desired changes can occur.

We have total and complete control over only one thing in life, our thinking. And learning to work with that is where your Personal Power begins.

THE THIRD PRINCIPLE – THE HERMETIC PRINCIPLE OF VIBRATION

"Nothing rests, everything moves. Everything vibrates."

This expounds the idea that motion is manifest in everything in the Universe, that nothing rests, and everything moves vibrates and circles.

Mental Transmutation is described as the practical application of this principle.

Everything that exists in our universe, whether seen or unseen, broken down into its most basic form, consists of pure energy or light, which resonates and exists as a vibratory frequency or pattern.

The mythos tells us that Hermes Trismegistus understood that the differences between different manifestations of Matter, Energy, Mind, and even Spirit, result largely from varying rates of vibration.

SCIENCE LATER CONFIRMED HERMES' THEORY

Science reveals that everything in the manifest universe is ultimately composed of packets of energy; quantised units vibrating at specific frequencies. Quantum physicists have shown that, although matter may appear to be solid when you look at it through a high-powered microscope so that it is broken down into its smallest components: molecules, atoms, neutrons, electrons and quanta (the smallest particles measurable), it is ultimately mostly empty space interspersed with energy.

To change one's mental state is to change vibration. The Ancestors understood this: "He who understands the Principle of Vibration has grasped the sceptre of power..."

HABITUATION

As your conscious mind dwells habitually on thoughts of a certain quality, these become firmly embedded within the subconscious mind. They become the dominant vibration. This dominant vibration sets up a resonance with other similar vibrations and draws them into your life.

FREQUENCIES AT WORK

Not only do we possess a frequency as matter, but our thoughts and emotions likewise create frequencies of their own.

Therefore, the vibrations around us can have an impact on our own overall vibrational frequency.

THE LEGEND OF THE SOLFEGGIO FREQUENCIES

In the 11th century, a Benedictine monk, Don Guido d'Arezzo, created a method of sight-reading music based on ancient wisdom, passed down in secret, which is said to have been the science behind Gregorian Chant.

Known as the Solfeggio scale, it was almost immediately recognised that the tones themselves seemed to have a remarkable influence over mental state, relaxation, ecstasy and even healing.

According to Dr Alan Watkins, a neuroscience lecturer at Imperial College, London, the Solfeggio frequencies on psychology and physiology – and numerous studies have come to the same conclusion.

They've discovered that the frequencies of sound and of colour both have a powerful and profound impact on the human mind, body and spirit.

In my own work, I've seen this proven, again and again, as patients with absolutely no metaphysical inclination or interests would come into my clinical practice, and as a naturopathic physician, I would introduce them to the pioneering healing work we've been doing for the past seventeen years, using sound frequency, and colour.

THE UNIVERSAL SOLFEGGIO FREQUENCIES

On the left are the nine Solfeggio frequencies. One the right is the systems impacted by that particular frequency, and the healing balance it creates. *(You can search for Solfeggio Scale on YouTube if you would like to hear the scale for yourself.)*

396 Hz – Liberating Guilt and Fear

417 Hz – Undoing Situations and Facilitating Change

528 Hz – Transformation and Miracles (DNA Repair)

639 Hz – Connecting/Relationships

741 Hz – Expression/Solutions

852 Hz – Returning to Spiritual Order

"Any expression of dis-ease – no matter whether you are injured or feel ill... whether you're feeling sad or depressed – is simply a symptom of a reduction in your natural vibration."

F. Gianmichael Salvato, N.D., Th.D., M.Sc.

THE FOURTH PRINCIPLE – THE HERMETIC PRINCIPLE OF POLARITY

The Principle of Polarity embodies the idea that everything is dual, everything has two poles, and everything has its opposite. All manifested things have two sides, two aspects, or two poles.

It recognises that opposites are identical in nature but different in degree and that all paradoxes may be reconciled.

The practitioner of magick or alchemy sees beyond the dualistic appearance, and works with the energy around the phenomena, transmuting causes and conditions to achieve the desired effect.

Thus, it is possible to change the vibrations of dis-ease into ease; hostility into harmony; fear into love, by simply recognising that they are two parts of the same whole.

It explains that there are two poles in everything and that opposites are really only two extremes of the same thing, the difference being only in degree.

An obvious example being hot and cold—both being temperature, varying only in degree. And that there is no clear moment when hot stops being hot and starts being cold and vice versa with no absolutes on either end.

The same can be said of 'light and darkness' 'hard and soft' 'big or small' and even 'love and hate.' With 'love and hate' there is no clear point where one emotion becomes another, or when it passes through 'like' 'dislike' or 'indifference.'

All notions of "opposites" are merely our perceptions of the degree on a spectrum. And the principle of Polarity exists to explain these paradoxes.

This principle is important to Hermeticists because it suggests we can change the polarity of such a degree of emotion, for example, by recognizing it is the same and choosing the degree which best suits our needs.

THE FIFTH PRINCIPLE – THE HERMETIC PRINCIPLE OF RHYTHM

"Everything flows, out and in; Everything has its tides; All things rise and fall; The pendulum swing manifests in everything; The measure of the swing to the right is the measure of the swing to the left; Rhythm compensates." (Initiates, 1908)

Sorry, White people, we all know you're going to be at a disadvantage when it comes to this one! (Laughingly just kidding... sort of.)

In all seriousness, the Principle of Rhythm is a universal law.

Winter always follows autumn. Spring always follows winter. Day will always follow night, and night will always follow day.

We see this in the tides, the lunar cycles and the seasons.

And we understand this immutable law in its direct relationship to the Principle of Polarity.

THE ALCHEMY OF EMPOWERMENT

Once the practitioner understands that apparent "opposites" are simply variant degrees of the same thing (i.e., dark/light, cold/hot, happy/sad), and recognises that the essential difference (polarity) is a matter of vibrational frequency...

And that the ebb and flow (rhythm) is an immutable law, which affects all things visible and invisible...

Then the practitioner can unlock the key to mastery of their experiences, by mastering themselves.

HOW ABOUT AN EXAMPLE?

This is Gianni. Gianni is an alchemist and witch, who understands that the "cycle of seasons" (a witchy way of expressing the Principle of Rhythm) is an immutable law.

He's kind of nice, pretty smart, and not too bad looking for his age...

Gianni is aware that the Principle of Rhythm applies to his mood and emotions as well.

 Some days, he is happy... Not a care in the world. Everything seems to flow nicely, and there are even moments of joy that would make Marie Kondo a little jealous.

But Gianni is mindful that not every day will be like this, as the Principle of Rhythm applies to all of the cosmos.

In fact, some days might just completely suck.

But Gianni knows that just as the ant thinks about the coming winter, while he enjoys the fun and frolic of summer, and the bountiful harvest of autumn, that same ant will survive the winter cold (having prepared with food and warmth during the harvest) by keeping his eye on the coming of spring.

Gianni knows the Principle of Rhythm dictates that the pendulum will still swing perpetually, to and fro, but that the practitioner of alchemy is able to "step off" at any point. We call this the Mental Law of Neutralisation.

When Gianni notices that his mood "pendulum" is headed toward the sad side of the spectrum, he recalls that both "happy" and "sad" are actually the same thing (mood). And that the only difference between them is vibrational frequency.

Therefore, he has the power to say, "No! I am not going to ride this pendulum to sadness."

He steps off the pendulum, and finds his point of innate equilibrium, which we call his "home frequency".

The Principle of Polarity and the Principle of Rhythm are the gateway to rediscovering our home frequency.

And our home frequency is the key to personal (magickal) mastery.

THE SIXTH PRINCIPLE – THE HERMETIC PRINCIPLE OF CAUSALITY (DETERMINISM)

"Every Cause has its Effect; every Effect has its Cause; everything happens according to Law; Chance is but a name for Law not recognised; there are many planes of causation, but nothing escapes the Law." (Initiates, 1908)

Your thoughts, behaviour, and actions create specific effects that manifest and create your life as you know it. If you are not happy with the effects you have created, then you must change the causes that created them in the first place.

Change your actions, and you change your life... Transform your thoughts, and you will create a brand-new destiny.

Causality is also known as "determinism". The concept of determinism is that a genetic connection exists between a phenomenon, through which one thing (the cause) under certain conditions gives rise to (i.e., causes) something else (the effect).

The essence of causality is the generation and determination of one phenomenon by another.

The Alchemist recognises that the Principle is Universal; therefore, Mastery requires understanding how this principle functions in the higher planes of existence, as well as within our own mundane physical plane.

The whole of humanity's history, of the history and birthing of the cosmos, knows no exception to the principle of determinism.

- Every thought creates an effect.

- Every word spoken creates an effect.

- Every action taken creates an effect.

To become the Master of your Destiny, you must master conscious creation.

As Above...

There are causations that exist outside the realm of our human control, such as conditions created by a plurality of causes in other realms or planes of existence, which contribute to the origination of phenomena within and across lifetimes.

So Below...

When we cultivate awareness that extends to all time and space, we begin to recognise that the witch's magick operates outside of time and space. Therefore, through personal mastery, awareness, and conscious creation, we can create the causes and conditions that transmute previous causes to manifest new outcomes.

THE SEVENTH PRINCIPLE – THE HERMETIC PRINCIPLE OF GENDER

"Gender is in everything; everything has its Masculine and Feminine Principles; Gender manifests on all planes."

--The Kybalion

The great Seventh Hermetic embodies the truth that there is "gender" manifested in everything--that the Masculine and Feminine principles are ever present and active in all phases of phenomena, on each and every plane of life.

This is not a new idea to most of us. We've grown up in a world that is familiar with the Chinese philosophy of *"yin and yang"*, the Hindu representation of *"Śiva-Śakti"*, the Goddess and Horned God of pagan lore, and in the scientific field, Jung's description of the "animus and anima".

It's important to note that the text of the Kybalion – written at the turn of the 20th century, immediately points out that this Principle has no reference to "the many base, pernicious and degrading lustful theories, teachings and practices," which the author recognises as "prostitution of the Principle".

This Principle is not about a *defective heteronormative ideology*, as many occultists and esoteric movements have attempted to promote.

It is a Universal Law, and perhaps the first clear and concise statement of the ***non-binary nature of all beings***, and indeed, all phenomena.

Within the text, gender has nothing to do with genitalia or sexuality. It is a reference to the process of conscious creation.

The concept put forth in The Kybalion states that gender exists on all planes of existence (Physical, Mental and Spiritual), and represents different aspects on different planes. Everything and everyone contains these two elements or principles.

Again, this Principle doesn't concern itself with what's between your legs. It's about every manifest phenomenon possessing the essence of the Divine Masculine and Divine Feminine in varying degrees. In other words, even physical gender is a *spectrum*.

The ***Feminine principle*** is always in the direction of receiving impressions. The Feminine conducts the work of generating new thoughts, new concepts and ideas, including the work of the imagination.

The **Masculine principle** is always focused in the direction of expressing, or sending out, and concerns itself with the "Will" in its varied phases.

IT'S ALL ENERGY...

Jung described the animus as the unconscious masculine side of a woman, and the anima as the unconscious feminine side of a man, with each transcending the personal psyche.

Today, we've begun to understand that things like gender function on a spectrum.

As witches, we recognise the Divine Order of the Cosmos and connect deeply with Nature Itself. This puts us in touch with a constant flow of both the Goddess and the God energy in all things.

The Kybalion explains why grasping these Seven Hermetic Principles is of importance to the Hermeticist, Alchemist and Practitioner of the Esoteric Sciences and Arts:

> *"Mind (as well as metals and elements) may be transmuted, from one state to another; degree to degree; condition to condition; pole to pole; vibration to vibration."*

APART FROM ONE ANOTHER...

We often talk about spirituality as a journey back to Divine Love — the Source and Only Reality. It is unwise, as I understand it, to imagine that this concept we call "God" or "Goddess" is somehow distinct and separate from us. Neither is there truth in that unhealthy dogma.

All of Creation is by nature the *Beloved One*, just as ice by nature is water. Apart from water, there is no ice... likewise, apart from one another, there is no Goddess or God.

If you want to experience the Divine, open your heart to see with the Eyes of the Beloved, the Indwelling Sacred in one another.

CHAPTER THREE – CONCLUDING THOUGHTS

Emmet Fox once said, "The Laws of Thought are the Laws of Destiny. Whatever you believe with feeling, that you bring into your life."

Throughout our history, witches have always sought out ways in which the fundamental spiritual, philosophical, and metaphysical truths of the ages could be stated in the plainest and most simple of terms so that we might harness their secrets and master our destinies.

But it's now time for us to start asking ourselves the difficult questions... the kinds of questions that make us a little uncomfortable. Because you see, those are the questions that inspire us to take action and reclaim the authorship of our own stories.

In his best-selling book, Return to Zero-Point, my dear friend and spiritual brother, Robert F. Ray writes:

"Are you truly happy with the way your life plays out? If so, you are a rare type of diamond. If so, do you have faith that it will always remain that way? I doubt you do. Have you not lost loved ones? Have you never had an argument? Have you not experienced a person in any capacity that was authoritarian, abusive, inflexible, or just plain difficult to deal with? Didn't you wish to change the relationship with that person, or want to get away from them, so you could accomplish things? Did you ever have an argument with a spouse that you wish never took place? Never got harassed, picked on, yelled at, or even swore at? These are everyday occurrences that people encounter; life in the 21st century." (Ray, 2011)

In any age, we know that actions that transform societies are driven by *key ideas*. Robert, who founded the Center for Inner Wisdom, in South Florida, continues:

"Is such a transformation possible? I think so, but in the end, once it has begun, we continue the transformation by continuing to work on ourselves. How can I transform society, or help it transform if I fail to begin with myself?" (Ray, 2011)

Healing is only possible when pain loses its value. Healing isn't really "fixing" something that is broken. It's the revelation of something that was "hidden" from our awareness.

I believe that by closely examining what we believe about specific things, people and circumstances in our lives, we can discover the opportunity to heal and correct those ideas which are not in alignment with Universal Truth. When we do this, our experience changes, and with it, the world around us is transformed.

A precept that works hand-in-hand with the recovery movement's *one day at a time* adage is the realisation that *for things to change, I've got to change; for things to get better, I have to become better.*

Horace writes:

> **Why do you hasten to remove anything which hurts your eye, while if something affects your soul, you postpone care until next year?**

I've decided to really focus on simplifying my mindset. It seems to me that much of what I experience as complication begins in my mind — subtly hanging-on to small circumstances, discomforts and interactions — allowing circumstance and situation to become the central, creative factor in my experience, rather than taking back that power myself.

Let's face it, I don't know if the people I have to deal with every day are going to become less passive-aggressive. I have no control over the backward mentality, the overall stupidity or the overwhelming neoconservatism of those who cling to the superstitions of the Abrahamic traditions, while criticizing my half century of service as a Witch, as being of their mythical devil.

But I have creative control, power and influence over how I allow those circumstances and situations to affect me.

Everything is transitory. Discomfort doesn't last forever. Thoreau challenges us to "learn to reawaken, and keep ourselves awake, not by mechanical aids, but by an infinite expectation of the dawn."

Just watch your thoughts. Whenever you have time just close your eyes and see thoughts and desires and memories moving on the screen of the mind. Be totally unconcerned.

Don't judge that this is right and that is wrong. If you judge you have already jumped in. If you say, "This is right," you have already chosen something, and the moment you choose you to become identified with it, you have become attached to it. You would not like it to go, you would like to keep it for yourself.

And when you say that something is bad you are pushing it away, you are avoiding it, you don't want it anymore. You don't want it even to be there on the screen; hence you have started fighting, struggling, and you have forgotten witnessing in all this.

Just be a witness: one sits on the bank of a river and watches the river flow by. There is nothing to judge, nothing really to say, but only to see. And if one is patient enough, slowly the traffic becomes thin. Less and less do thoughts come on the screen and sometimes for moments there is nothing on the screen and you are facing an empty screen.

Those are the most precious moments of life, those intervals when thoughts are not there, you are simply **present**.

The seer is there with nothing to see. Those are the moments of purity, innocence, those are the moments which can be called divine. They are no more human. You have transcended humanity in those moments.

Slowly those moments become bigger and bigger, and one day it becomes such a simple process that whenever you want to you can go into that interval, into that *thoughtlessness*. Fully aware yet thoughtless – that is meditation. And that is the only thing that can liberate you from all kinds of psychic bondage. The only thing that can bring peace to you, and bliss and the truth of your own divinity.

MASTERY OF THE MIND BEGINS WITH BECOMING QUIET

Meditation is essentially training our attention so that we can be more still, more aware, more in touch with our True Nature. Our True Nature is Pure Awareness.

From this Pure Awareness springs forth the Bodhicitta Mind — Wisdom and Compassion — the basis for transforming the world, by transforming ourselves.

The more we deepen our practice of meditation, the more we manage to cultivate that serene stillness, the greater our sense of remarkable resourcefulness and the awareness of our intricately woven interdependence, which allows us to lead lives that are organically more free, more energetic, and more full than ever before.

Our path is a path of stillness. One learns to hold the Śakti, rather than allowing oneself to be controlled by it. While we recognise that this calls for greater spiritual maturity and commitment, we must always allow space for those whose paths call for more or less stringent or focused practice.

As Sharon Salzberg reminds us:

> "Meditation may be done in silence & stillness, by using voice & sound, or by engaging the body in movement. All forms emphasize the training of attention." (from *The Power of Meditation: A 28-Day Programme for Real Happiness*)

Not long ago, two of the students I felt showed the most promise for guiding the future of our Order chose to leave the teaching. They claimed that I was too hard on them and that my consistently calling them on their shit was "abusive". From a Westerner's perspective, they were probably right. And if we were founded as a Western Order, perhaps my approach would have been a little more New Age, Airy Faerie, Unicorns and Rainbows.

But that's not who we are. And it's not what this teaching is about.

I will always miss those two students and know that if they would have dedicated even 15 minutes a day to their spiritual practice, sitting in quiet meditation, their journeys would have been dramatically different. Their experience of "harshness" and "abuse" might have been viewed as the concern and guidance that it was intended to provide.

If more of my students practised meditation even fifteen minutes a day, I wouldn't have to ask people to support the social justice work and service to the poor that we undertake. They would open their hearts and their wallets regularly because they would recognise this as THEIR work... THEIR community. THEIR Order.

Through meditation, our understanding of the true nature of things — seeing things as they really are — becomes the ground of wisdom. And from that fertile ground, our practice takes root and blossoms, like never before.

APPENDIX

SEVEN-POINTED MIND TRAINING PRAYER

I bow to the Spiritual Friends of the Supreme Vehicle,

Source of everything good in Samsara and Nirvana.

By the gracious Lama's blessings, may my mind be purified with the three kinds of faith.

By the gracious Lama's blessings, knowing how hard to obtain and how easily destroyed is this precious human life. In all my actions according to their karmic effect, may I try to do what is right and avoid what is wrong and develop a genuine determination to be free from Samsara, as I train in the preliminaries.

By the gracious Lama's blessings, may I purify the untruth of duality into the space of voidness and practice the profound exchange of my own and others' happiness and suffering, meditating continually on the two aspects of Bodhicitta.

By the gracious Lama's blessings, may I see whatever adverse events and sufferings befall me as tricks of the evil spirit of ego-clinging and use them as the path of Bodhicitta.

By the gracious Lama's blessings, may I condense my lifetime's practice into a single essence. By applying throughout my life the five powers of pure determination, pure practice, accumulation of merit, purification of obscurations, and prayers of aspiration.

By the gracious Lama's blessings, when everything arises as the antidote to ego-clinging and my mind finds freedom with happiness and confidence, may I take all adverse circumstances as the path.

By the gracious Lama's blessings, may I keep my promises, be free of hypocrisy, have no partiality, and little outward show. Protecting the commitments of mind training as I would my own life.

In essence, by the gracious Lama's blessings, may I genuinely train my mind according to all the precepts which further the two aspects of Bodhicitta and attain realization of the Supreme Vehicle within this very lifetime.

By the merit of this heartfelt aspiration to practice the Seven Point Mind Training, the essence of the minds of the peerless Lord and his disciples, may all beings accomplish enlightenment!

Index of Terms

100% responsibility, 14, 15, 57, 71, 72, 79, 93, 114
abhiśeka, 81, 82
Alchemy, i, ii, iv, v, 5, 123
Aspiration, 49, 51
Bodhicitta, 4, 19, 24, 48, 49, 78, 79, 137, 140, 141
Bön, 1
Buddhism, 1
Buddhist, v, 1, 2, 6, 10, 16, 17, 30, 31
Cause and Effect, 6
Cekawa, 3, 9
Chekawa, 7
Chekawa Yeshe Dorje, 8
Chekhawa, 8
Correspondence, 6, 112, 114
Dreams, 30, 32
Familiarisation, 49
Four Reminders, 10
Gender, 6, 128
Hermetic tradition, 2, 102
Hermeticism, 3, 96
HUMAN BIRTH, 10
IMPERMANENCE, 10
Jamgön Kongtrül Lodrö Thayé, 10

Kybalion, 2, 4, 6, 7, 96, 105, 106, 128, 129, 130
Langri Tangpa, 8
Lojong, 3, 8, 9, 20, 41
Mentalism, 6, 105
Mind Training, 3, 11, 12, 20, 40, 42, 51, 56, 60, 61, 64, 66, 73, 141
Morningstar, iv, v
mystics, 2
New Thought, v, 1, 96, 106, 110
Pimander, 97
Polarity, 6, 121, 122, 123, 125
Prisca theologia, 99
psychic, 1, 136
REALITY OF SUFFERRING, 10
Reproach, 49, 50
Resolution, 49
Rhythm, 6, 122, 123, 124, 125
Rimé, 11
Seven-Pointed Mind Training, 2, 3, 4, 27, 140
THE DEFECTS OF SAMSARA, 10

BIBLIOGRAPHY

Chodron, P. (1994). *Start Where You Are: A Guide to Compassionate Living.* Boston: Shambhala Publishing.

Hall, M. P. (1988). *The Secret Teachings of All Ages.* New York City: Penguin.

Hauk, D. W. (2013). *The Emerald Tablet of Hermes.* Ocean Shores: Merchant Books.

Initiates, T. (1908). *Kybalion.* Chicago: Yogi Publications.

Pel, N.-K. (1992). *Mind Training like the Rays of the Sun.* Library of Tibetan Works and Archives.

Rabten, G. (2001). *Advice from a Spiritual Friend.* Somerville: Wisdom Publications.

Ray, R. F. (2011). *Return to Zeropoint.* Fort Lauderdale: Zero-point Continuum Publications.

Rinpoche, C. T. (1981). *Training the Mind and Cultivating Loving-Kindness.* Boston: Shambhala Publications.

Rinpoche, D. K. (1993). *Enlightened Courage: An Explanation of the Seven-Point Mind Training.* Ithaca: Snow Lion Publications.

Rinpoche, J. K. (1987). *The Great Path of Awakening: An Easily Accessible Introduction for Ordinary People.* Boston: Shambhala Publications.

Tangpa, L. (2012). *Eight Verses for Training the Mind.* Lotsawa House.

Wallace, B. A. (1992). *The Seven-Point Mind Training.* Ithaca: Snow Lion Publications.

Yenlak, K. (n.d.). *A Concise Lojong Manual.* Nepal: Marpa Kagyu Dharma Preservation Center.

Manufactured by Amazon.ca
Bolton, ON

45113033R00095